LEADER'S MANUAL
Hymnal for Catholic Students

Gabe Huck

Robert J. Batastini

Carole Eipers

Diana Kodner Sotak

Robert H. Oldershaw

Richard Proulx

LEADER'S MANUAL
Hymnal for Catholic Students

Liturgy Training Publications • Chicago
GIA Publications, Inc. • Chicago

Acknowledgments

This book and the *Hymnal for Catholic Students*, which is supplemented by an accompaniment edition and audiocassette recordings of the music, are a joint project of GIA Publications of Chicago and Liturgy Training Publications of Chicago. These materials were planned by an editorial committee whose members were Robert Oldershaw, Mary Prete, Diana Kodner Sotak, Michael Silhavy, Robert Batastini of GIA and myself. I am grateful for the direction and excitement these people generated. Specific thanks are due for parts of this volume to: Robert Oldershaw and Diana Kodner Sotak for initial work and continuing insights for the liturgy outlines in chapter 5; Carole Eipers for suggestions toward classroom preparation for the liturgies in chapter 5; Richard Proulx for the section in the appendix on children's voices; Robert Batastini for the section in the appendix on helping people sing; Robert Oldershaw for the index of music.

Gabe Huck
Liturgy Training Publications

The English translation of the Directory for Masses with Children © 1973, International Committee on English in the Liturgy, Inc. All rights reserved.

Design by Ana Stephenson. Cover art by Helen Siegl.

ISBN 0-929650-10-7

CONTENTS

PART ONE

When You've Got a Liturgy, What Have You Got?

What does it mean to "get the children ready for a liturgy" or to "get a liturgy ready for the children"?

It means, "Watch out!" It means, "Pitfalls abound!" And it also means that you are being trusted with something at the center of what it is for us to be the church.

First, both things do need to be done. Children need to be prepared for the liturgy. And the liturgy needs to be prepared for the children. People have found all sorts of shortcuts and that is understandable. Few have had the opportunity to study or read about liturgy. Most of the time we are happy if we hold the interest of the children, if they can remember some of the homily the next day, if they say something pleasant afterwards.

The purpose of this book is to help teachers and other leaders become at home with their role in preparing the children and the liturgy.

The first step involves some notions about what sort of activity this liturgy is.

Is the liturgy one thing and prayer something else?

Yes and no. Sometimes in the liturgy we pray. But think of all the sorts of things *in addition to praying* that we do just at that one liturgy we call the Mass. For example, we listen to the scriptures. That may be prayer*ful*, but it really isn't prayer. We gather money for the church and for the poor. We bring bread and wine and place them on the altar. We exchange the sign of peace. The *prayer* elements of this liturgy usually come after the person presiding says, "Let us pray," or "Let us give thanks to the Lord our God." They come also in the litany of intercession when, over and over again, we say, "Lord, hear our prayer."

Prayer has a much bigger life than liturgy, and liturgy has a much bigger life than prayer. We pray at some regular times (like rising, at meals, going to bed) and at some unusual times (being sick or being with someone who is sick, times of fear or danger or rejoicing). Prayer is our address to God. It is our conversation toward God. Sometimes in that conversation we speak in unison with lots of other people, sometimes we speak alone. Sometimes we speak with words, sometimes just with thoughts, silence, contemplation, feelings.

We could imagine one big box that has in it all the ways we pray. Liturgy would be another box. Some part of the liturgy box would be inside the prayer box. Some of liturgy is prayer. Some of prayer is liturgy.

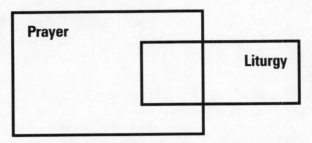

We can still speak of the Mass as a prayer, but it is helpful if we sense that at the liturgy we do many sorts of things, prayer included. And it helps also to realize that prayer can be done in a great many ways and at a great many times.

When liturgy isn't prayer, is it just a ritual?

The question is phrased that way because we often think that way. "Just a ritual," we say, because ritual has a bad name among us. It means the things we do without thinking, the automatic things, the habits that we often would like to break in order to bring some freshness and some life in their place.

Ritual has a bad reputation. Yet if we are going to understand what liturgy is, we are going to have to give ritual a good name.

When we talk about the rituals of Catholics, we mean that rituals are the things people do over and over, the things that they know by heart. These rituals may be gestures (like the sign of the cross or genuflecting), they may be words (like the Our Father or the Amen), they may be postures (like standing for the gospel) or movements (like the processions), they may be days kept in special ways (like fasting on a day of Lent or feasting on Christmas), they may be wearing special garb (like a wedding ring, a vestment, a cross or medal), they may be the whole way we approach an event like marriage or death.

Such rituals do a wonderful task. Little by little, they tell us who we are. They can do this because we know them by heart. They come to us then as naturally as breathing, sleeping, eating. Certainly they can be done "by rote," on automatic pilot—and that is where rituals get their sometimes questionable reputation. But when a group takes care of their rituals, handles them carefully, gives them room to thrive—then the rituals do their work. The sign of the cross every morning, the fasting and charity every Friday, the celebration of eucharist every Sunday, the Advent and Lent and Christmastime and Eastertime every year, the Angelus every noon—all of these identify us as members of this Catholic tribe. They are precious little images of what it is to be a Catholic.

So we can clean up the reputation of rituals. And we can take another look at the question above. Yes, the Mass is a ritual (and not "*just* a ritual") or perhaps many rituals joined together. From the first moment to the last, when we celebrate Mass we are doing an order of things we well know how to do. The sign of the cross is just moving arm and hand—yes, but here, in this pattern we know well, it is identifying ourselves, "blessing" ourselves, marking ourselves with the sign of God's love and victory. So it is with the whole of this ritual: From the scripture readings to the communion, we do very familiar deeds, deeds Christians have been doing through all their generations.

We can show this with more boxes. Ritual is a big box that takes in all sorts of things like seasons and feasting and fasting and special garb and vigil lights. And it also takes in the liturgy of the church—all of the liturgy. Ritual takes in some ways of praying, too, both at the liturgy and apart from the liturgy.

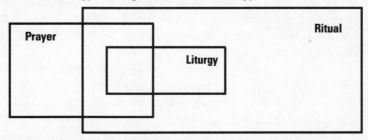

What difference does it make that liturgy is ritual?

A huge difference. So often we seem to think of liturgy as something that somebody else does *for* us. So we go to Mass hoping to be inspired, uplifted, "get something out of it." Or we plan a liturgy for children and what is in our minds is keeping them interested, almost entertained. We take a sort of performer/audience approach to liturgy and hope the reviews are good.

But when we see what sort of thing liturgy is, then we really can't do that anymore. A ritual isn't something you watch. It isn't something that is entertaining. It isn't there to inspire or uplift an audience.

Ritual is something that the people do. It belongs to everyone. It is done by everyone. Everyone knows it by heart. Some have particular responsibilities and they serve the others by taking this work or that work, but they are not the *doers* and the others the *watchers*. A ritual like the Mass is done by all the people there. That is what the Catholic church has been about in the generation since Vatican II. The Constitution on the Sacred Liturgy proclaimed that full and conscious and active participation by all the faithful was their right and their duty because they are baptized. That is the way the Directory for Masses with Children would have us act in preparing the liturgy that children celebrate together with some adults in the school setting.

Full and conscious and active participation: How does it happen?

It happens only when one is on familiar ground and glad to be there. There is no such participation in a liturgy that is made up from scratch or a liturgy that is "planned" with various ideas to be communicated or themes to be stressed. Liturgy is ritual. Ritual, for all its dangers, is where full and conscious and active participation can happen. Ritual means familiar ground. It means a time when the participants are at home, know their way, are free to take part because they *aren't* being taught or entertained or inspired. Ritual means that this is mine to do, mine as one of this community. Ritual means what comes over and over again, ways of acting together that are the same ways our Christian ancestors acted, ways that they handed on to us.

If we know how to do this liturgy fully, actively and consciously, then perhaps we can invite children into a liturgy that is worthy and well prepared. It comes to making the rituals of the church, Mass included, a home—familiar ground. Adults and children know how to sing such liturgy and we have good melodies with which to sing it. We know how to listen to scriptures read in our midst, how to acclaim and how to join in holy communion. It gets into the muscles and the heart.

Where do the ministers at the liturgy come into this?

Ministers are first of all members of the assembly. They are there as all of us are: to take part in our liturgy. That is why any arrangement of the church or room that suggests an audience and a stage is going to create a false sense of what is happening. It makes the ministers into performers. The arrangement should help us see and feel how everyone—including those with special roles to take—is a member of the assembly.

Those who step from the assembly and exercise a ministry must be persons who have prepared to do that ministry well. Ordinarily that doesn't happen when a person is a lector only once. It happens when a person has a chance to get to know lectoring, to be on familiar ground as a lector. Those who preside at liturgy, those who lead the song, those who read, those who are ministers of communion—all should be able to get the flow of the liturgy into their bones so that they are free to give all their attention to being good servants and not just good at remembering what comes next.

We have prayer, ritual, liturgy. How does each fit into the school community?

Prayer is all the ways the individual and the community address God. Little by little, a Catholic school will be teaching prayer to students. Some of the ritual prayers of our tradition will be taught: the Our Father, Hail Mary, Gloria, Confiteor. Some ways of praying spontaneously, even some ways of praying without any words at all will be talked about.

Ritual refers to all those ways our faith is expressed by us in symbols, symbols that are repeated over and over in various rhythms of time. So a school, like a home, will teach the rituals of the church: the seasons with their traditions, the regular ways of fasting and almsgiving, the gestures like the sign of the cross, kneeling, taking holy communion.

And then liturgy. All of the liturgy is ritual, but not all our rituals are liturgy. For the Roman Catholic, the liturgy is those rituals that the whole church holds so dear and so vital that their celebration is described in the church's documents and books. This does not mean that they are unchanging, but that their alteration is not to be done lightly or by people acting on their own. They belong to the church. As such, the liturgy is the deed of the church united with Christ. When we speak of the church's liturgy, we mean not only the eucharist, but the sacraments, the liturgy of the hours, various blessings and seasonal celebrations. It should always be kept in mind that the normal way of celebrating the liturgy is with the parish community, especially at Sunday eucharist. Any other celebrations of the liturgy must be related to this.

Which liturgies are appropriate for the school setting?

The *Hymnal for Catholic Students* suggests that there are three times, each with its own rhythm, when the liturgy is to be part of the school life.

First, the *Hymnal* has a simple form of morning and of evening prayer: "Prayer to Begin the Day" and "Prayer to End the Day." Morning Prayer and Evening Prayer from the church's official liturgy have been adapted to the school day and to use with children.

Second, the *Hymnal* has a rite of penance or reconciliation. This is taken from the church's ritual book and is the form in which many persons celebrate this sacrament together.

Third, the *Hymnal* provides the student with the order of Mass. This is done in two ways: "Sunday Mass" and "Masses on Other Days." The order for Sunday Mass simply presents the normal way that Catholics celebrate their liturgy Sunday after Sunday. The "Mass on Other Days" offers the order of the liturgy adapted for those times, usually not a Sunday, when the assembly is mostly children. The commentary on the Mass makes the *Hymnal* useful in the classroom for continuing catechesis on the liturgy.

By providing many psalms, hymns and other music, as well as a selection of Catholic prayers, the *Hymnal* is also a resource for prayer services when Mass is not celebrated.

What is the role of the assembly—whether adults or children—at Mass and at other rituals of the church?

This is the question that the whole liturgical renewal has been about. At the heart of it is how we understand the liturgy. Do we think it is something that somehow works all by itself? Do we think it is something that is meant to give those in attendance a spiritual boost, or insight into some problem, or solace and warmth? Do we see it as an hour to try to make religion interesting to children?

If we take any of those approaches to liturgy, what happens is this: We make liturgy into an us-and-them situation. Some people do things, and some have things done to them.

This was, in fact, the problem that the bishops of the world addressed at the Second Vatican Council. For hundreds of years, the liturgy had been there for the ordinary people to watch, to follow along sometimes. We might think of it this way: The liturgy could make a difference to the person-in-the-pew, but the person-in-the-pew couldn't make a difference to the liturgy. The first task of the bishops at the Council was to write what is called the Constitution on the Sacred Liturgy. There they confronted this us-and-them approach to liturgy: "us" being one side of the communion rail, "them" being the other.

A generation later, with lots of things changed, us-and-them remains a problem.

We still have something less than the "full, conscious, and active" participation that forms the heart of the document written by the bishops at Vatican II:

> The church earnestly desires that all the faithful be led to that full, conscious and active participation in liturgical celebrations called for by the very nature of the liturgy. Such participation by the Christian people as "a chosen race, a royal priesthood, a holy nation, God's own people" (1 Peter 2:9; see 2:4–5) is their right and duty by reason of their baptism. (Constitution on the Sacred Liturgy, number 14)

That is the child's role—everyone's role—at the liturgy. "Role" is not even the word. The Council speaks of "right" and "duty." So in introducing children to the liturgy, in celebrating the liturgy with them at Morning Prayer or at Mass, we are forming them to do their duties and to exercise their rights as baptized Christians.

What does a children's liturgy look like then?

It looks like something that the children know how to do. That is the key. It means that the liturgy isn't put on for them, but is theirs. It means that those responsible are helping these baptized children take hold of what is their right and duty.

What we and they need to know is how to enter into such a liturgy with song and gesture and word. What we and they need to know is how to listen to the words read from the scriptures, sing psalms and offer prayers. What we and they need to know is how to attend as the table is prepared and then give thanks and praise to God in acclamations to the words of the eucharistic prayer spoken by the presider. What we and they need to know is how to take our place in a communion procession, eat and drink of Christ's body and blood. What we and they need to know is how to take leave of this time and place and one another.

That is the premise of this book and of the *Hymnal*. It is not based on a children's liturgy being created from scratch every time, created in order to keep the attention and interest of the children. It is based on this: that it is the right and duty of children to celebrate the liturgy. We approach this liturgy not asking, "What can we do with it this time?" but, "How can we and these children make it our own?" That means that we approach with a great respect for the simple order of the liturgy, for its own sort of timing, for its special days and seasons.

This book and its *Hymnal* are rooted not only in the more general documents about the liturgy that have come from Rome since Vatican II, they are rooted also in one very unique document that is fully accessible (as near to you as the appendix of this book): the Directory for Masses with Children. This was published in 1973, approved and confirmed by Pope Paul VI. It is short and it is readable and it sets down with great clarity what we should expect about children and the liturgy. It also goes into detail on exactly the sort of liturgies we are discussing in this book: liturgies celebrated with many children and a few adults. It would be well to go no further in your reading until you have read the Directory.

Isn't the liturgy supposed to speak of the here and now, of this community in this place at this time?

Exactly. But it is the *way* liturgy does this that we have often lost in the rush to be interesting and inspiring. Understanding that the liturgy belongs to the "ritual family" can be of great help here. Rituals aren't rituals if we make them up every time. Rituals do their work because we don't have to fashion them anew. We can do them by heart and thus we open ourselves to a different sort of transformation. If we have to think of a new way to say good-bye to our spouse each morning, we will probably end by not saying good-bye at all. If we say good-bye with a kiss, we don't show any great originality or inspiration, but that kiss given day after day, year after year, becomes a part of us. Certainly, it can also become a lie, an empty moment. That is the danger of ritual. Like a lot of good things, it can be misused. We have to take care.

What our rituals at their best are meant to do is show us how to be the people we became at baptism. When, little by little, we can make the rituals of the church our own, they rehearse us in being baptized people. In the words that we say, the melodies that we sing, the processions that we walk, the gestures that we make, we learn to be Christians. The simple sign of the cross is such a ritual. Just a movement of the hand, a shape traced on the body. Like that good-bye kiss, though, it can be shaping us into something—the image and body of Christ.

To go back to the question: Yes, liturgy speaks to the here and now, but not in the way we often think. It speaks because we who do the liturgy are here and now. The liturgy we do is the liturgy we have received and made our own. That's the only liturgy we have. If *we* are there—fully, consciously, actively—liturgy is going to be about here and now—and about all that is eternal.

What resources are there for those who work with children's liturgies?

The books and records and tapes are many, but approaches and quality vary greatly. Some materials come close to treating children's liturgies as entertainment or as show-and-tell. Some songs make of the liturgy something trivial. Often one finds an attitude that says: Liturgy is whatever we want it to be. With that premise, one is left to search each week, each month and each year for the new and different. Liturgy is challenged to compete with television. It can't. It shouldn't. This approach asks too little of both liturgy and children. It finally deprives children of that foundation for Christian life that only full participation in the church's liturgy can make. So, let the buyer beware!

The basic resources for anyone who takes responsibility for the liturgy, whether with children or adults, are those documents by which the directions for liturgical renewal have been established. They are neither numerous nor lengthy. Careful reading of these, and returning to them often, grounds an individual and a team or committee in the church's striving to renew the very source of Christian life. The basic documents are these:

CONSTITUTION ON THE SACRED LITURGY. This was adapted by the bishops of the world as the first work of Vatican II and it remains the charter for the liturgical renewal. Much of what it calls for has been begun, but the vision of renewal and the understanding of liturgy expressed here continue to nourish all who would work with the liturgy.

GENERAL INSTRUCTION OF THE ROMAN MISSAL. This is a somewhat lengthy document that translates the vision of the Constitution on the Sacred Liturgy into the reform of the eucharistic liturgy in the Roman rite. The General Instruction sets forth the order, the options, the requirements of the Mass. It is always found in the front of the sacramentary.

LECTIONARY FOR MASS: INTRODUCTION. The lectionary is the book of scripture readings for the Sundays, weekdays and feast days of the year. The Introduction to the 1981 revision of the lectionary is an excellent background for understanding the liturgy of the word, the ministries involved and the principles by which the scripture readings were chosen. Those who work with lectors and those who help to select readings should be thoroughly acquainted with this work.

GENERAL NORMS FOR THE LITURGICAL YEAR AND CALENDAR. This is a brief document that outlines the seasons and feasts of the liturgical year.

DIRECTORY FOR MASSES WITH CHILDREN. This is the application of all the above to Masses with children. It will be found in its entirety as an appendix to this *Manual*. The principles and norms of the Directory should be studied and discussed among teachers and all others responsible for Masses with children.

The above documents originated in the Roman office that oversees the liturgical renewal of the church. The following documents are the work of the bishops of the United States.

MUSIC IN CATHOLIC WORSHIP. The integral place of music in our liturgy is outlined along with a description of the kind of music appropriate at various places within the Mass. A supplement, Liturgical Music Today, applies these principles to the sacraments and other liturgies.

ENVIRONMENT AND ART IN CATHOLIC WORSHIP. Though the stated goal is to treat matters of space and the objects used in the liturgy, this short document is probably the best possible introduction to any work with the liturgy. It places the assembly at the center of our concern.

All of the above will be found in a single volume, *The Liturgy Documents*, published by Liturgy Training Publications (LTP). Other resources from LTP that will be helpful include:

The Welcome Table: Planning Masses with Children by Elizabeth McMahon Jeep and others. A variety of concerns are addressed from the viewpoint of the catechist and the clergy. The book includes a detailed planning chart for use in understanding the Mass and preparing each liturgy. This book includes several sections that are about and are addressed to those who preside at children's liturgies.

Liturgical Calendar. A large multicolor poster prepared each year for use in the classroom and home. It shows all the seasons and the feasts of the year.

At Home with the Word. An annual publication that takes each week of the year and gives the Sunday readings along with reflections and activities. Seasonal prayers are included.

Catholic Household Blessings and Prayers. This book contains daily prayers and traditional Catholic prayers as well as short rites for use in the home. Many of these blessings would also be appropriate in the classroom. This prayer book is prepared and published by the bishops' conference for the United States.

Welcome Yule! (for Advent and Christmastime) and *Paschal Mission* (for Lent and Eastertime) are weekly calendars filled with ideas and activities. They are published each year.

CHAPTER TWO

Some Rules for Liturgy with Children

Repetition is not only OK, it is required.

We can learn about repetition from little children. Does a child want a new story read every night? Does a child want a different place to go to bed every night? The same old words, the same old place—these are a kind of a home, territory physical and spiritual where the child delights, set free by the familiar.

Liturgies and all rituals require repetition. A person or a group has to know their liturgy as the child knows the beloved bedtime story or the room and the bed. Then it is a ritual.

Some of our rituals we do know that well: the sign of the cross and "Bless us, O Lord," for example. We should be just as much at home in the liturgy of the Mass. It becomes ours to do through repetition: its words and its melodies, its rhythms of reading and singing, its patterns of prayer and communion. These are like a familiar room to us.

We undermine this when we treat the liturgy as something we create each time from scratch. Instead we should trust our liturgy. The Roman liturgy, which we have received from our ancestors in the faith and which has been renewed in the last generation, has a wonderful sense of joining things that change and things that remain the same. Even more, it has a structure in which the changing and the unchanging meet. That structure, like the structure of a proper Thanksgiving dinner or of a school pep rally, is something we are to grow up with. We make it our own. We know in our bones how alleluia leads to gospel, how "for ever and ever" leads to "Amen." And when such is truly ours, then we are shaped by it. When we don't have to look at a piece of paper to know that "We lift them up to the Lord" is our answer to "Lift up your hearts," then lifting up our hearts to the Lord will begin to be a way we live our lives.

Certainly repetition is a two-edged sword. Those who would prepare the liturgy for children and children for the liturgy have to be students of repetition. They have to watch the rhythms and how they work. They have to know the things that are always the same at every Mass, those that are only for a season like Lent, those that are only once a year (for a feast like All Saints). Most of all, they have to respect and handle with great care the way that the Mass structure itself is rendered familiar and accessible to the children in every celebration of the liturgy.

Those who minister come from the assembly to serve the assembly.

The assembly is everyone: all the baptized and the catechumens who do the liturgy. The presider is one member of the assembly. The reader and the musicians and the communion ministers are members of the assembly. The assembly is the body of Christ, this church, gathered together. The liturgy that we do together requires that some members of the assembly do this or that special service for the whole assembly. The presider at the Mass is one ordained to exercise this leadership, this presidency of the assembly. But the presider is first of all just one of the baptized, a member of the assembly. Other members of the assembly, because they have special gifts and have received training in the use of these gifts, will take on special tasks. But all the tasks are so that the whole assembly can do the liturgy.

This can be especially difficult in liturgies with children. If children are to fulfill any of the ministries, they must be qualified to do so. The job of the reader is not simply to be passed from one to another in alphabetical order. For each ministry, certain skills are necessary and much practice is required.

The variety of ministries makes it nearly certain that every child can be trained in some ministry. Yet liturgy consistently celebrated well will show everyone that simply being a member of the assembly is the most dignified and demanding role of all. Those who preside or do the readings or play music or take on any special tasks at all will always be expected to show in their expression and their participation that they are first and last good members of the assembly.

Sometimes it is better that adults do some of the ministries, such as reader or leader of song. It still holds true: First and last, the adult is a member of the assembly. The Directory for Masses with

Children (in paragraph 24) has a strong point to make about any adults who are present for Masses with children: "These should be present not as monitors but as participants." No spectators are allowed at our liturgy. When adults minister, it is all the more important that they prepare well for their special role and practice with other ministers as necessary so that the liturgy does not become a performance.

Liturgy is something sung.

A liturgy done in the speaking voice is like a pep rally where the cheers are whispered. It isn't a pep rally anymore, of course. A spoken liturgy is hardly liturgy.

We have gotten fairly accustomed to thinking that there are times at liturgy when we sing. It would be better if we thought that there are times at liturgy when we don't sing—but mostly, we sing. The assembly sings their liturgy. That is the way things are supposed to be. They don't sing *during* the liturgy or *at* the liturgy. *They sing the liturgy.* This is one of the most basic and powerful things we can do in preparing children to be the assembly. It can gradually change the whole way we adults think about and celebrate Sunday Mass.

Why is the liturgy sung? Why is "Happy Birthday" sung? Why is "Go, team, go" shouted with a rhythm to it? There are some jobs that the plain speaking voice can't handle because it isn't the words alone that are important but *what they have to do.* They have something to express. They have something to carry out. Think of the crowd roaring at a football game: something to express, something to carry out. So we need our singing so we can go higher and lower, faster and slower, than speaking. And there are other reasons: We need time to dwell in some of the words. To rattle off "Holy, holy, holy" makes no sense. And we need melodies that let the texts get inside us, melodies that bring the words and the action back to us. That is shown when we cannot simply recite the words to a hymn, but we have to start humming it, singing it, and then the words come.

Within the liturgy of the Mass, there are some things that should always be sung. First are the acclamations. These include the Sanctus and the memorial acclamation and the great Amen. All of these are part of the eucharistic prayer in which the assembly is participating by listening and joining in to acclaim that prayer. In the forms of the eucharistic prayer for Masses with children, these acclamations are even more frequent. Other acclamations at Mass include the Alleluia that leads to the gospel.

Second, the psalm that comes during the liturgy of the word is to be sung, at least the refrain that belongs to the assembly. The psalm is not a reading; it is its own thing, a bibilical song. It is the best way we have to learn to pray. It needs a measure of quiet surrounding it, and it needs a sense of contemplation, of peace. The words and melody should be wedded. Psalms may also be used at other times in the liturgy, especially in the communion procession.

Third, we sing the litanies. Litanies are a form of prayer where the people have a very simple line, but by its repetition it gives a shape and a vitality to the whole prayer. In a litany, the overall rhythm is most important to the way the prayer is made. It is one thing to say "Lord, have mercy" in a speaking voice after a series of petitions, and it is quite another thing to sing those words. The intercessions or prayers of the faithful are a litany. The penitential rite is usually a litany. Before communion there is another litany, the "Lamb of God."

Fourth, we sing in procession. Often this means the entrance procession or the recessional. But the one consistent and most important procession is the communion procession. Without music here, the procession turns into a lineup. Without music, it is that much harder to sense that here is something we do together. The voices tell us that.

If it is the liturgy that is being sung (and not just people singing while the liturgy takes place), then these various moments in the liturgy don't sound like one another. The sounds are not interchangeable. What is right for singing as a psalm will not work as an acclamation. The music that is called for by a procession will not do for the litany of intercessions. Each assembly needs a very limited repertory of each type of music, strong selections that will stand up to repetition and will draw all the assembly into singing their liturgy.

The liturgy is like a dance: The whole body must be used.

Aidan Kavanagh has pointed out what damage pews—which were added to places of worship only relatively recently—did to the liturgy of Catholics (see his book, *Elements of Rite*, page 21). Pews made us into an audience. They lined us up and sat us down. They put us in rows and lined up the rows, just like a theater. They made an obvious distinction between those in pews and those free from pews.

Even when we are in a space without pews, we seem to carry the pews with us. We have not learned how physical the liturgy is, how much movement and space it requires. This is not to make a case for dance within the liturgy. It is only to say that the liturgy is already a dance: an order of motions. And the prime mover/moved is the assembly, ourselves.

Our posture is the first part of this. What are the times for sitting, for standing, for kneeling? These are not meaningless directions to be followed. Part of getting the liturgy into our whole being, making it our own, knowing it by heart, is letting posture be quite natural. Thus, sitting is a position for listening and for reflecting; it is receptive, comfortable. And standing is a position for action, for attention and for respect. Kneeling is the position of adoration and of contrition. (Note that we are in a transition time regarding posture during the eucharistic prayer. Some assemblies kneel, some stand. Both postures can be said to be appropriate, but the more ancient and fitting would seem to be attentive standing around the altar.)

With children as with adults, the posture should flow from attention to the liturgy—and not from a spoken direction: "Please stand." Such directions are almost never in place. Sometimes the cantor or presider may need to indicate an invitation to rise with a gesture of the arms, but when the liturgy comes to belong to the assembly, even that sort of direction will seldom be necessary.

More important for presider and other ministers is that they model these postures well. *How* one sits or stands or kneels matters. Students can learn that postures at liturgy are not just arbitrary. In a classroom discussion or even in a homily there is time to reflect: What does it mean to stand? What does it mean to kneel or to sit? What is the attitude that the culture conveys toward these postures and what is our attitude?

Those who prepare liturgies for children need to be attentive to the matter of posture. For the most part, this simply means a consistent approach (and not deciding that this week, because the gospel is a bit long, we'll sit for it). It will mean also that the seasons may make some slight difference (in Lent, for example, kneeling for some time at the penitential rite; during Easter, not kneeling at all).

Liturgy is handling and gesturing.

The "dance" that is any liturgy is done by everyone. Those who take roles as presider, cantor, lector or minister of communion have to move and use gestures and carry things. These must never be simply casual and offhand actions, nor should they give off the scent of artificial piety. Difficult as it is in our culture, liturgy would have us move with reverence: being at home in our bodies in the presence of the Lord and one another. We do not move and act here in a different way for the sake of being different. Rather, the way we move and act here is some brief vision of how we would have ourselves be all the time. The reverent way we treat this bread and this wine, this book and this human being, is just exactly the way we say God's reign is to be. It is that reign we try to bring day by day in the ways we act with things and one another.

This means that for all ministers, adults and children, practicing alone and rehearsing together are important. This does not make liturgy a performance. On the contrary, this is the only thing that can keep it from being a performance. Only when the ministers can move at ease because they are so certain and so trained in doing their work well will they become "transparent": We see through them to what this is about. The carrying of a book, the swinging of a censer, the cantor's gesture to begin singing, the gospel reader's kissing of the book, the presider's open arms for prayer, the communion minister's offering of bread or cup—all such ordinary gestures, as well as simply walking and standing, should be done well as a matter of course. These are the small things without which the liturgy will never become the deed of the assembly.

The assembly, too, has its gestures: the sign of the cross at beginning and end, the cross on forehead and lips and heart at the gospel, the bowing of the head during two lines of the Creed, the greeting of peace, the extended hands for bread and cup at communion. Each of these can and should be the matter for reflection and even practice; sometimes this would be appropriate within the homily (see, for a wonderful example, the short homilies for children by Balthasar Fischer, *Signs, Words, and Gestures*, Pueblo Publishing Company). We seem to have mixed feelings about such gestures as folding the hands and striking the breast (as during the Confiteor), but these gestures have a rich tradition and still seem capable of contributing to a worthy liturgy. We have a great self-consciousness, but in fact such simple gestures can free us of an undue self-consciousness when all do them together.

Liturgy is not about how we feel. It is about who we are and whose we are.

What has been said about gestures just now makes this point important. Much is made today of feelings and of the individual's great importance. When Christians enter upon their liturgy, however, all of that must be balanced with something else. The liturgy is what the church does. If I do the liturgy, I do it as a

baptized member of this community of baptized persons. In a sense,
I play a role that is only partly mine now, the role of a member of
God's reign. The liturgy does not exist so that I can get my feelings
expressed. Rather, it rehearses me in the feelings I ought to have.

We speak of folded hands, peace greetings, loud acclamations,
gestures of penance like kneeling, and all such things. It is never a
matter of: Do this if you feel like it. Hard as it may be for persons of
this culture to accept, the liturgy would have us do things whether
we feel like it or not. At liturgy, we play like we are in God's reign,
as we are but only a little. This is true not only of the eucharist, but
of Morning and Evening Prayer, the seasons, the sacraments. When
we praise God in the morning it is not because we *feel* that praise
but because we are baptized people and in the name of all creation
we are here to praise God.

All that being said, we can begin to glimpse how the liturgy is
filled not simply with emotion but with passion. Look at the words
we sing in the psalms and hear in the scriptures, look at the lives
we celebrate on feasts, look hardest at the very core of the eucharist.
In the eucharistic prayer we speak as passionate people about
creation and sin and God's relentless love. The climax of Catholic
liturgy is the eating and drinking of Christ's body and blood, a deed
that holds and little by little reveals a multitude of human passions.

Children cannot be taught this. They can only sense it in their
community and grow into it.

Liturgies are filled with processions.

As Aidan Kavanagh points out, liturgies find us ever on the move.
We begin with an entrance procession. That is not the procession of
the presider and other ministers through the assembly. The entrance
procession is really the assembly's procession into the place of their
liturgy. It may indeed conclude with the formal procession of
presider and others, but first attention goes to this: How does the
assembly assemble? Is there care taken that the place be entered
with some sense for what we are going to do here? Too often we are
satisfied simply to get everybody in place in whatever way, then
"begin." But we have already begun—when we started toward this
place. That is the procession that counts. What attention goes to it?
In a school setting, it may even be possible that this be a true procession
with singing and ordered movement from classrooms to church.

Within the liturgy of the word, we have the gospel procession
in which special honor is paid to the gospel reading. This is a
procession made possible by the alleluia-singing assembly. Even if

it consists only of the presider moving toward the book, it is a true procession. In this one person's movement, we are all moving—slowly, with excitement, with praise, with awe and even fear—toward the words of the gospel. There has to be room for that in the way the assembly regularly does its gospel. If, on great feasts, candles and incense are part of this procession, and if the book is held high and carried into the midst of the assembly, then we manifest and discover even more of what our lifelong procession is about.

The procession that brings the bread and wine to the table is very simple and should ordinarily not be complicated by bringing other objects forward. Other things prepared especially to be part of the liturgy can very appropriately be incorporated into the entrance procession discussed above. But at this moment, the liturgy calls for the table to be set (and, when appropriate, an offering to be taken from everyone—and this, too, is a gesture of the liturgy—for the church and the poor). This is a quiet moment within the liturgy. With reverence, the bread and wine are brought forward and placed on the table. In some settings, the whole assembly moves to a position of standing around the altar when the bread and wine are in place.

The communion procession is the most important of the liturgy. And it is for us the most difficult. It helps to recall the very simple thing that is happening. This bread and wine, become for us the body and blood of Christ, are shared in the assembly that just joined in the eucharistic prayer, then the Our Father and the peace greeting. That assembly comes forward—not to help themselves from plates and cups left on the table—but to be served one by one by ministers of plate and cup. Every liturgical direction points toward the importance of this act being done as a procession. A procession is the ordered and spirited moving of a community. It looks and it feels quite different from the line at the bank or the grocery store—or the moving lines of a military march. When you are in a procession, you are part of a community. Everything should support this: the music, the order of coming forward, the manner and the number of the ministers of communion. It is a time to sing and there is need for song, but it must be song that supports a procession, a communion procession. Such music exists, but it must be found and used. Some of the Gelineau psalms, for example, are excellent with their brief refrains. These are easily memorized but still beautiful after singing them in hundreds of processions.

The last procession is again the assembly's. Especially in Masses with children, there is seldom a convincing reason for the presider and other ministers to leave by themselves. They might join in the general going out of everyone, sometimes with song, other times with instrumental music or silence.

Entering, leaving and the communion procession should be matters of great concern, of good habits and of periodic evaluation. The entrance and the recessional may be given special forms during the seasons of Advent, Lent and Eastertime—but even here, a community should strive for consistency from year to year. The communion procession should be a steady and strong part of every liturgy. Special instructions should never be necessary. The whole communion rite, from the Our Father to the prayer after communion, is perhaps the most fixed part of the Mass. Every member of the assembly should be so at home in its flow and its movements that the whole rite belongs to all those present.

The liturgy has times of silence.

Silence has been somewhat neglected in practice, though it is there in the liturgical books: after the invitation to pray, after the readings that precede the gospel, after the homily, after communion. Each silence is linked to what came before. At some point, children need to consider each of these silences. Classroom preparation and even an occasional homily can do this. As a society, we are uneasy with silence. Children may be less so than adults, but we like to believe they are less inclined to silence than even we are. Like so much else, it may be that they are ready; we are the ones afraid.

Most of the time, silence needs stillness. That would mean that the presider isn't fidgeting with a book, the cantor isn't trying to communicate something to the organist, the acolytes aren't having a conversation. Stillness. No movement. And long enough for the silence to settle in and take hold. Experience will show how long the silence should be, but a minimum of 30 seconds would seem right. The practice should be fairly regular so that the length of the silence is taken for granted and everyone is thus freed from wondering about it. For this to happen, those who are responsible for ending a silence (the cantor, who will begin the psalm after the silence that follows the first reading, or the presider, who will end the silence after communion by inviting, "Let us pray") must have a good and common sense (not one cantor with one notion and one with another) of the length of the silence.

Like almost everything else at liturgy, silence doesn't have a chance at the Mass unless it gets practiced somewhere else. Where there is the practice of regular morning prayer in the classroom, silence should have some small place. This can follow the invitation "Let us pray," and be after the short daily reading from scripture.

If the teacher or the homilist should happen to talk with children about what the silence is for, then teacher or homilist will have to have something to say, something from their own experience. It may be as simple as suggesting that the invitation "Let us pray" is not a call for thinking up all sorts of things to pray for, but rather a chance for quieting the mind and heart, for sensing the presence of others in their silence and so being ready to make one prayer as the church. It may be suggesting that the silence after the reading may be for reflecting on one single word or one phrase from the scripture we just heard.

The Directory for Masses with Children says this about silence: "[The children] need some guidance, however, so that they will learn how, in keeping with the different moments of the Mass (for example, after the homily or after communion), to recollect themselves, meditate briefly, or praise God and pray to God in their hearts." (number 37)

Comments should be few, brief, prepared.

Sometimes those who prepare liturgies and lead liturgies with children feel that they have to say many things. This comes from good motives: wanting the children to understand, wanting to be friendly, fearing that the liturgy by itself will be too obscure. What happens too often, however, is that the liturgy is overexplained or that a running commentary replaces the liturgy. This has to be resisted. The Directory for Masses with Children, like the General Instruction of the Roman Missal, mentions a number of times when some additional words by the presider may be in place. It does not mean to say that such words are needed at every liturgy or at every juncture where they are allowed.

Comments should be carefully prepared beforehand so that they stay short. If such comments proliferate, the message is clear: Liturgy is like a class and the presider is a teacher. The presider (whether the priest at eucharist or another adult at daily prayer) labors always under the burden of remembering that this liturgy belongs to the church and especially to this assembly. It is not a stage or a podium.

Presiders have a responsibility at every liturgy to study and prepare all the texts they are to speak: especially the opening prayer, the eucharistic prayer, the prayer after communion. These are formal texts, some far stronger than others, but all needing careful attention if they are to be truly heard by the assembly.

At eucharist, the word of God is to be a foundation.

The Directory for Masses with Children notes that the readings from scripture may be reduced but scripture must always be read (see numbers 41–49 for the Directory's lengthy treatment of this subject). There may be only two readings, even on a feast day, or even only one (in which case it must be from the gospel). Assigned readings from the lectionary may be shortened or other scripture readings may be substituted if the assigned readings would not be helpful for the children. The Directory suggests that the conference of bishops prepare a version of the lectionary especially for Masses with children (this task has been under way in the United States and such a lectionary will be available in 1990).

The Directory is clear that the readings at Masses with children are not to be paraphrases of scripture but rather translations that have been prepared especially for use with children. The Directory also notes that length is not the criterion to be used in deciding on a reading but rather the "spiritual advantage that the reading can bring to the children" (number 44).

All of this attention to the readings is by way of underlining their immense importance to our liturgy. The introductory rites achieve their purpose when an assembly of children can sit down to listen to scripture. The scripture that is read is read not for study and not for the edification of individuals, but it is read for the church. We listen as the church. These are the words we build on, the foundation. When they are brushed aside because something else is on the agenda of the day, when they go unheard because the reader was not prepared or the sound system not working or the delivery too cute, then we are left foundationless. There is nothing for us to stand on. Without a foundation, how are we to intercede, to celebrate eucharist, to go out and live?

For every liturgy, great effort must go into the preparation of the reading. Whether child or adult, the expectation is the same: many days of struggling with the reading, some real rehearsal and critique, prayer, delivery that draws attention not to itself but only to the word. Because this is difficult to achieve even with the simple situation of a single reader, it should not be assumed easily or often that the readings can best be handled by groups or with special dramatic settings.

There is no place in the liturgy of the word for readings not from the scriptures, except when the homilist includes such a text within the homily.

The liturgy is celebrated in a fitting place.

The Directory lists a few criteria for the place where the eucharist is to be celebrated with children. It notes that the primary place is the church, but "within the church, a space should be carefully chosen if available, that will be suited to the number of participants. It should be a place where the children can act with a feeling of ease according to the requirements of a living liturgy that is suited to their age" (number 25). If someplace other than the church is chosen, it "should be appropriate and worthy of the celebration."

Note that the concern here is for a space that will allow *this particular group* to celebrate the liturgy. A space that will hold 800 is not appropriate for 80. But perhaps a space within that large space is. Some stability is necessary. All that has been said of repetition would require being at home in the space. Even when another space is regularly used for liturgies with children, the children should be introduced to all facets of the church building itself, the place where they come on Sundays for liturgy.

The experience of the last two decades has been that we too often choose very ordinary spaces for children's Masses, or else simply go into the parish church with no effort to use the space wisely. The former case—using classroom or gym or hall or cafeteria—very often works against building any sense of reverence. We bring the habits of classroom, gym or hall to liturgy when, in fact, we are meant to bring the habits of liturgy to all these other places. But if we never learn the habits of liturgy, we have nothing to bring. It is not a matter at all of some spaces being "holy" and others not. It is a matter of understanding the great difference the environment makes to the liturgy. It is exactly the same understanding that should keep us from a decision to use the church building without any effort to make it an environment suitable for the children to celebrate their liturgy.

The objects and furnishings of the liturgy are to be worthy.

Very few things are needed for our eucharistic liturgy. Consider the list of basics:

- the book of scriptures (lectionary)
- the book of prayers (sacramentary)
- the bread and its plate

- the wine and its cup
- the table on which the vessels are placed
- vesture of the presider
- the ambo (podium, reading desk) where the scriptures are read
- seating for assembly and presider
- a processional cross and candles

The rule should be: Take care that these are worthy of their task and are used with reverence. Take care also that the community established a steady practice regarding each of these things. The temptation is always to neglect these in favor of what is secondary.

The list does not include books or other participation aids for the assembly. Most often something will be needed and it should never be something careless or shoddy. When the liturgy belongs to the assembly, as it ought to, books or other aids will only be needed when hymns are called for. Psalm refrains, acclamations and litanies will be known by heart.

Those who have responsibility for furnishings and objects and for their arrangement should know thoroughly what is said in *Environment and Art in Catholic Worship*. This is the 1978 statement of the United States bishops. Establish the basic setting, the assembly gathered first around the word and then around the table. Make certain that the books, vessels, bread and wine, vesture and other items listed above are habitually worthy and are being well cared for and handled. Then attend to those other objects that may be needed for particular liturgies. Constant attention will be needed to the basics. Our tendency seems always to go off on doing mobiles or banners or Advent wreaths or Christmas trees and to make do with shabby lectionaries, wafer-thin bread, no wine for the assembly. Back to the basics!

Liturgy does not happen in a void.

The liturgies that we celebrate with children should be in great continuity with other regular occurrences in their lives. There are three special things to be noted here. First, we learn to do what is expected of us at liturgy in our other rites. If liturgy asks that we sing, we must be learning to sing somewhere else. We won't learn it just at liturgy. We will learn because song is something we do together at Morning Prayer in the classroom or at meal prayer in school or home. If liturgy asks that we keep silence to prepare for prayer, it can expect that we have learned to do this at bedside prayer before sleep or at the short prayer that concludes our day together. If liturgy asks that we listen well to the scriptures, it is because we practice such listening at other times of prayer and at other times when the Bible is opened and read at home or school. If liturgy asks that we praise and thank God and pray to God for the needs of the world, it can do so because we are people who practice this kind of praying every day. The church is filled with ways that all these things can happen regularly, but we have been slow to make them our own. Instead, we tend to let the liturgy bear all the burden—which it cannot.

Second, the liturgies we celebrate with children have a context of catechesis. For too long we have had religious education on one track and the liturgy on another. In recent years, good efforts have been made to bring them together. In part this is reflected in the great emphasis on scripture in our religious education. It is sometimes just another step to see how the way that the church reads the scripture together, at the liturgy, can give shape to the content of religious education at all levels. In a setting where the approach suggested in this book and its *Hymnal* has been adopted, children and adults will not come to the liturgies "cold." They will have been preparing in little ways through the previous weeks: hearing a bit of the scriptures, learning the tunes of hymns or refrains and discussing their words, discovering the stories of saints and the traditions of the seasons. Such catechesis builds and deepens each year for the child moving through the grades.

Third, the liturgies are to have a sort of echo to them. Their tunes are heard at daily prayer in the following days and weeks, their homilies are discussed and expanded. And not only that, but the deeds of the liturgy—the thanks and remembering and the breaking of bread and the eating and drinking, the ashes and the Easter candle and the blessings and the peace greeting—all these become the lens through which we understand the faith and share that faith in the formation of children. This is perhaps what the church means by "mystagogia," that word that described how the early Christians used Eastertime to "unfold the mysteries," to let the newly baptized ponder how their very lives are summed up in baptism and in eucharist. Those who teach children are mystagogues also, charged to draw from the liturgy the strength of our own lives and to return with the children again and again to that liturgy for understanding how we are to live.

All of this—learning little by little through daily prayer how to be the assembly, catechetical preparation for every liturgy and a mystagogical remembering of each liturgy—are the making of a wholeness of which liturgy is the center.

Liturgy in the school setting is to be in continuity with the parish liturgy.

The church's primary and normal existence is the parish. The liturgy of the parish, and that means above all else the Sunday eucharist of the assembled parishioners, is the heart of parish life. All other celebrations of the liturgy are secondary to and dependent upon that Sunday liturgy. This has been the way of the church from the beginning. First this took shape in the Lord's Day gathering of the baptized around the bishop; the scriptures were read and the eucharist was celebrated. Later, local groups gathered around a presbyter delegated by the bishop. That is our practice still.

A school or any other expression of the parish does not create a liturgical life apart from that of the parish. It lives by the Sunday eucharist. When the parish enters into the season of Advent or Lent, the school is part of that entry. When the parish is preparing catechumens for baptism, the school is part of that preparation.

The direction of liturgy in the school, then, should never be to create its own independent liturgical life, to act as if it existed in a void. The parish liturgy may not be as solid and strong as desired. That should not keep the school from being an example of liturgy well celebrated. But even in doing this, the school needs to remember and show in some visible ways how it draws its life from the Sunday eucharist and the seasonal observances and the initiatory practices of the parish.

Liturgy with children has dignity, clarity and simplicity.

In the Directory for Masses with Children, we read: "The priest should be concerned above all about the dignity, clarity, and simplicity of his actions and gestures" (number 23). Those three nouns—dignity, clarity, simplicity—might be good ways to think about and even to measure our progress in celebrating the liturgy with children.

Dignity is from the Latin word for "worthy." Everything that we do should strive for this worthiness. As the Directory notes, this would mean avoiding anything that is childish. Other words might be added to this one. Avoid what is casual, trivial. All of that is unworthy. Dignity has nothing to do with putting on styles that make the word "phony" pop into the observer's mind. Dignity is rather in the elimination of all phoniness. Dignity is putting on something else, our amazing baptismal garments, our person clothed with Christ. Do we achieve ever greater dignity in our liturgies?

Clarity is akin to this. It does *not* mean that we make the liturgy into a game: "Now, children, when I break the bread it means just this or that." Clarity is rather in breaking that bread so that the hundred and the thousand things that it means will be dawning on presider and assembly alike. Clarity is breaking the bread so that the breaking becomes the meaning of our life. Clarity is attention to the liturgy's own patterns and priorities and not confusing them with our own. Clarity is in the striving for that regular practice of a liturgy that children and adults know to be their own work for God's reign, a liturgy it will be somehow in us to do and even to need to do. Such clarity in liturgy rules out any effort to impose one's own agenda or personality on the rite.

Simplicity is the burden and the genius of our Roman rite. But how do we keep simplicity from turning into a poverty on the one hand, or being rejected in favor of someone's complex agenda on the other? Thus we run the gamut from liturgies that are merely a running through the words and gestures to liturgies that make it difficult to know if the eucharist was celebrated at all. Neither approach trusts our simple Roman liturgy. The challenge to those who prepare and celebrate with children is to seek after that simplicity. Know what's important in doing the liturgy—that's bound to lead to simplicity.

CHAPTER THREE

The Calendar of School Liturgies

This chapter offers an understanding of the church's days, weeks, feasts and seasons. This understanding is basic to the specific liturgies to be presented in chapter 5. The specific notes that make up the bulk of this chapter need to be understood in light of three principles.

First, the school community lives within the parish community. This was stressed in chapter 2. It is repeated here to remind us that the school is not "a church" but a part of this parish church. Schools, like any other parts of the parish, live by the parish's Sunday eucharist. Thus, we don't set out to create a calendar from nothing. We are part and parcel of this parish. The Sunday liturgy, not our school liturgy, is primary. The scriptures of Sunday should surface within the school's life. The psalm and other songs of Sunday should not be absent from the school's singing. The way the parish is observing Lent is of the greatest importance in beginning to think of how the school will observe Lent. Likewise, patronal feasts and days of ethnic or diocesan importance should have their impact on the school's calendar.

Second, the school lives within its own calendar. We might want to ignore this, but we do so at great risk. The school has a year that begins in the fall and ends in the spring, usually during Eastertime. The school begins a long holiday before Advent has ended and only resumes in the midst of Christmastime. Within the school's year there are various times of special observance or special stress. When we begin to plan the calendar of liturgies for a school, the slate is not blank. It has not only the parish year already on it, but the school's year.

Third, our approach to a calendar of school liturgies should not be, at the start, a discussion about when the eucharist can be celebrated. Begin, rather, with a sense for seeking those days when the school as a whole (or perhaps several grades together) ought to join for a liturgy. Only later face the question of whether that should be or can be the eucharistic liturgy, or whether it should be or must be a liturgy of the word or Morning Prayer or Evening Prayer. Any of these last three lend themselves to marking special days. The gift and skill for presiding at the liturgies of large groups will come increasingly from nonordained persons in the next years. These gifts and skills must be developed. If they are, then by choice or by necessity we will keep many of the great days of a school's calendar with a liturgy other than the eucharist. A community's liturgical calendar is not about the availability of ordained persons but about the Christian formation of its members. The Sunday eucharist is clearly central, vital to that formation. But for other days, we have a tradition that is rich in noneucharistic liturgy.

With that said, we can look at the makings of a calendar.

Begin at the center: the Triduum.

And what is that? The Triduum (just a word from the Latin for "three days") is that time from the night of Holy Thursday to the afternoon of Easter Sunday. The revision of the church's calendar in 1969 (following the directives of Vatican II) restored these days to their primacy in year and in life. They are called the Paschal Triduum, the "Easter Three Days." They are about the solemn and joyful observance of the Lord's passion, death and resurrection— kept not as historical commemoration but as present to the world now, in our midst, especially in the baptism of the catechumens. As they die to sin and put on the Lord Jesus, we are present to our own baptism.

All liturgy preparation begins with the Triduum and so must that of the school. And here it becomes clear just how bound the school must be to the parish, for the only celebration of the liturgies of the Triduum is in the parish, never the school. In fact, the church has a practice that says a parish should have only one liturgy on Holy Thursday, only one on Good Friday, only one Easter Vigil. Why? Because on these days above all others, the unity of the parish is to be manifest as all gather for one single prayer.

So the first step in a calendar for the school year is looking to the Triduum. When will it be? Because the date of Easter is set according to sun and moon (first Sunday after the first full moon after the spring equinox), that date can vary from late March to the third week in April. From those three days, our year spreads out in both directions.

The Triduum has to be more than three days on a calendar. It has to become a center to the lives of teachers and other adults. That is the point of beginning here. How do *we* (faculty, staff) think about and observe these three days? How much a part of our consciousness and prayer are the catechumens who are with the parish all through the year that leads to their baptism at the Vigil? How do we think about our own baptism: just a ritual years ago or the ongoing effort to die to sin and put on Christ? A school cannot be Catholic, let alone build a calendar of liturgies, if it shies away from what the liturgy is celebrating. So such things have to be confronted. We will be stronger for doing it.

The 50 days of Easter come next.

After the Triduum, the church marks down Eastertime: 50 days from Easter Sunday to Pentecost. This is looked upon as one great Sunday (it is about one-seventh of the year), a single day that, like Sunday, is somehow outside of the normal cycle of life and partakes of eternity. Such an Eastertime is a figment of the imagination until we have restored the Easter Triduum with its baptisms. But even then, it takes both determination and imagination: How are we to keep days of delight, 50 of them? What does this do to the school calendar? It tells us to ponder how Eastertime may permeate our last weeks of each school year and how that may be expressed in one or more school liturgies.

The other occasions of this time of year must be seen in the perspective of Easter. First communion, of course, is quite at home in Eastertime (any other time of year should be by way of exception). But the keeping of any special end-of-the-school-year liturgy or any special Marian liturgy in May should be prepared in full light of Eastertime. Once those 50 days are on the calendar, let them be the home of anything that happens. Catechesis at every level can consider the liturgies celebrated during the Triduum, especially the Vigil, and draw from it much to teach and discuss. The water of baptism can be present in the classroom, and the sign of the cross with holy water part of Morning Prayer.

The 40 days of Lent prepare for the Triduum.

The calendar then goes backwards from the Triduum. The season of Lent begins on Ash Wednesday and ends on the evening of Holy Thursday. It is to be a time when the catechumens enter into the final preparation for baptism and when all the baptized are called to remember what it means to be baptized and to do penance. This is a wrestling match of a season, 40 days like those of Jesus in the wilderness, when we summon all our strength and try to face up to the evil that gets inside us and that is certainly at work in our world. We get ready for it with a wild carnival, then engage in our best fasting (of all kinds), almsgiving (of all kinds) and prayer (of many kinds). All of these can pick up on or begin a variety of communal expressions for Lent's fasting, alms and prayer in the life of faculty and students. Here, too, is the occasion for catechesis on how charity (alms) and discipline (fasting) come into a Christian's life. This is exactly the context for considering the moral life: the fall, the commandments, the invitation of Jesus, the practices of the church.

If the parish has catechumens preparing for baptism, the children should be aware of them (especially from the lenten Sundays where the catechumens are "elected" for baptism and "scrutinized"). The names of these people should be in the daily intercessions. Sometimes there will be children from the school who are catechumens. It may be appropriate to celebrate some of the rites of Lent (such as the presentation of the Lord's Prayer and of the Creed) within the school community.

The days of Lent go on the calendar and are to be defended with a fierceness. Too much—from St. Patrick's Day to spring break—gets in the way of this quite short season. Soon there is nothing left. Lent's work depends on its having a running chance. The school may decide that at this one season there is to be a weekly liturgy—if not of the whole school, then of groups of classes. The first of these, of course, is the liturgy of Ash Wednesday. This can well be a parish liturgy (that is, one that is listed as open to any parishioner), but prepared especially for the children. This is one occasion that makes it quite clear how our gestures must be allowed to speak for themselves. The strength of the blessing and marking of ashes should not be lost in wordy explanations.

On the night of Holy Thursday we simply leave Lent behind and enter the Triduum. The school alone can do little apart from the parish as a whole to be certain that the Triduum is kept with strong liturgies and with fasting and prayer and then rejoicing and feasting in every life and home. What the school can do, for the children and their families, is to build a strong sense that Lent has truly prepared us, and now we enter the Triduum. One part of this might be a simple liturgy during the day on Holy Thursday, before school adjourns for Easter.

Our calendar now has 40 days plus 3 days plus 50 days: the whole paschal season, a quarter of the year. Within this, we should be marking those days when the school will celebrate liturgy together. And we should also be establishing the framework that will help Lent, Triduum and Eastertime be something real—heard and smelled and tasted and touched and spoken and sung—in the life of the school.

The other great season is Advent and Christmastime.

This season begins with the First Sunday of Advent and lasts through the feast of the Baptism of the Lord (usually the Sunday after Epiphany, but occasionally the Monday after Epiphany).

What do we say about a season that begins in the aftermath of the Thanksgiving holiday and gets tangled in the culture's secular Christmas (the "Christmas" that began just after Halloween and will end about noon on December 25)? Not only that, but the school is probably not in session for fully half of the days of Christmastime.

Though it may sound unrealistic, the calendar is the church's and so it is ours. All the beauty and wisdom of Advent is worth a thousand strategies for holding off the Christmas carols and decorations. But it has to be pretty much across the board: a policy upheld by all. It can't be done unless someone goes after Advent, finds its tunes, its art, its stories, and shows to everyone: These are worthy of our full attention and in fact they are the only way to get to Christmas at all. Any other Christmas is "let's-pretend."

Then in whatever days the school has of Christmastime itself there can be a liturgy of Christmas. These might be days between New Year's and Baptism of the Lord, but they should be time for the Christmas parties and decorations and songs and lights.

Again the bond between parish and school matters greatly. How does the parish keep its Advent, wait for its Christmas, then celebrate mightily until the Epiphany? Though the feast of the Presentation of the Lord on February 2 is not a part of the Christmas season, its story does bind it to that season and, as the observance called Candlemas, it should be celebrated by the church. This is a day to mark on the school's calendar.

So now our calendar has seasons and liturgies marked for the winter-spring season, and for the weeks before and after Christmas.

All the rest is Ordinary Time, the time for feast days.

The weeks outside Advent-Christmastime and Lent-Triduum-Eastertime are the weeks "of the year" or "Ordinary" Time, the weeks that are simply numbered: "The Second Sunday in Ordinary Time," "The Twenty-second Sunday in Ordinary Time," etc. On the

Sundays of all these weeks, the church has a very simple way of choosing what scriptures to read. One year, we read through the gospel of Matthew, chapter by chapter, on the Sundays. Next year, Mark. Next year, Luke. Then back to Matthew. Likewise, the readings assigned to the weekdays of Ordinary Time move continuously through various books of the Bible. But in Ordinary Time (much more than in the seasons of Advent-Christmastime or Lent-Triduum-Eastertime) the weekdays are also occasions for celebrating the great feasts and the little feasts: feasts of the Lord, of Mary, of angels and saints.

The next step in a school calendar, then, is a look at the feasts of the year. This begins with the general calendar of the church. In a generic way, chapter 5 has done that and suggests days for liturgical celebrations. A school should not be satisfied with this, however. Each place needs to look also to the local calendar: What saints are important in this community? What feasts bring to the community the suffering and the rejoicing in their own past as Christians? These may be days like Saint Charles Lwanga, Saint Wenceslaus, Our Lady of Guadalupe.

The suggestions made here were chosen not only for their great importance to the universal church, but also for their place in the year's calendar. They are days outside the great seasons, days within the school year:

> September 14: The Holy Cross
> September 29: Michael, Gabriel, Raphael
> October 4: Saint Francis of Assisi
> November 1: All Saints

Finally, in each classroom, some lesser days are added to the calendar. These may be the feast days of the patron saints of the students and teacher. When these days come around, some effort should be made to learn and tell the stories of these saints.

The calendar of the school and classroom also needs to record other days that will have importance in the lives of these students: school holidays, national days, anniversaries, equinox and solstice, election days, exam days.

Put your calendar in place.

The church has acted and still acts as if it expected that the keeping of seasons and the marking of days of celebration and of penance would form Christians. We often seem not to trust such things: Instead of letting our teaching and art and song flow out of the liturgy, we have tended to turn the tables so that liturgy becomes just another piece of teaching. Thus the search for "themes" or "topics" of the liturgy can go on as if the church—ourselves—did not already possess this wonderful calendar.

Trust the calendar. That is the invitation of this book. Let the several seasons and the feasts, with their eucharists or other liturgical celebrations, be central to the life of the school. This cannot be done in a year, but it can be begun. And it needs the repetition of the years to do its work.

For this to come about, more than well-prepared celebrations of the liturgy are necessary. There needs to be a rhythm of preparation/celebration/reflection going on within the individual teacher and student and within the community as a whole. Most often this will be seen in the classroom through topics of discussion, the songs, the art projects, the scripture and stories and poetry read in the days and weeks before one of the liturgies. And it will be seen also in the things talked about after the liturgy. Teachers need resources for this—the first of which is the liturgy itself with its texts and its music—but more than resources, they need a commitment to the work and beauty and power of the liturgy and of its expression in daily practice.

Go from calendar to practice.

1. Publish the calendar widely and well. This is not just a list of dates on a piece of 8 1/2 × 11 paper, but first of all a great work filling a central wall or bulletin board. It will need some way of indicating the movement of time through the year. Each room needs to construct its own version of this. On such a calendar it is not so important that every day be noted equally, but that the seasons be clearly given great space and that the feasts that will be celebrated with liturgies stand out. Taking care of the calendar through the year says that this was not a meaningless wall decoration but is the shape of life around this community.

2. Agree on responsibilities. The work of liturgy is hard work. Those who will prepare the various ministers and those who will prepare the space (all year or for a single liturgy) should know early who they are and what is expected of them. These are not tasks to be randomly passed around but are for those with experience and skill. Those with the basic task of taking the suggestions in chapter 5 of this book and bringing them to life in this school will need to work well ahead (in the first year, then build on that experience each year that follows). They should see as one of their prime responsibilities the communication of information about readings

and songs and gestures so that the teachers working with the children can be informed and enthused as they prepare the children.

3. In the preparation of the liturgies, go back again and again to the principles of good liturgy. These can be gleaned from the various documents through which the modern renewal of the liturgy is slowly coming about. See the list that begins on page 11. These are our grounding. The liturgy is not whatever we would make of it. It is something we have received, something that is to live for us and our children, and something we shall hand on. These documents bring us close to the best and clearest the church can be when talking about its liturgy. This can and should be supplemented by regular review of the structure of the eucharist as it is described in chapter 4.

4. Don't be afraid to write things down. Each school (as each parish) needs a very clear set of guidelines: This is the way we celebrate the eucharist at St. N. School. Such guidelines should allow for the seasonal and feast day variations, but they should set down basics. For example:

• The sign of the cross is always made to begin the liturgy.
• A silent time of at least 30 seconds always follows the first reading from scripture.
• The acclamations are always sung: One melody is used for the feast days, another for the seasons.

And so on. These should be simple, direct and enforced (if that is not too strong a word).

5. After a liturgy, be certain there is a good written description of the liturgy. Put with it an evaluation so that next year things can be even better. Do this evaluation very soon. It need not be painfully probing: just helpful notes for next year.

6. It is best if one person has the responsibility and the authority to be coordinator of liturgy for the school. The purpose of this is to avoid many of the things that can go wrong when responsibility is not fixed. Remember that we are talking here of coordinating, not inventing.

Children and the Church's Liturgy

The preceding chapters have offered an approach to liturgy and the calendar for all who work with children. The chapter following this one will look in detail at each of the liturgies, offering notes on background and classroom preparation. This chapter offers an outline of the Mass. It applies what has already been said about the workings of the liturgy and it serves as the framework for all that is said in chapter 5 about specific liturgies (even those that are proposed as liturgies of the word rather than eucharistic liturgies).

We will "walk through" the Mass. Readers know it well already (that is presumed), but it will help to step back and try to see it in a fresh way. Though much of what is said could be applied to the parish Sunday liturgy, the focus here will be Masses at which children are present in greater numbers than adults. The Directory for Masses with Children (DMC) will therefore be used throughout.

There is a second purpose for these notes. Those teachers who use this manual will be, in many ways, preparing children to participate in the Mass. In doing this, teachers will be able to use the *Hymnal for Catholic Students*. The *Hymnal* is not only a book for participation in the liturgy. It is perhaps even more a book for *preparation* for such participation. Thus it offers the children, in the section called "The Mass," an overview of "Sunday Mass" and an overview of "Mass on Other Days." These are meant primarily for use in the classroom as children work with their teachers to learn the Mass. "Sunday Mass" contains those texts that the children should be learning by heart as they grow up participating in Sunday Mass. It also offers a very brief commentary on the Mass from the viewpoint of those who do the liturgy, the assembly. "Mass on Other Days" is the basic outline for all the eucharistic liturgies that the children will celebrate as a class or school. The notes here are somewhat longer. Both outlines of the Mass should help the teacher in preparing the children for liturgy. Neither teacher nor student needs to be a scholar in the liturgy, but Catholics do need to take possession of their liturgy, to know well what it is they have received, to know its shape and its movement, its words and its gestures.

So what follows can be taken as the "teacher's manual" for working through the material found in the *Hymnal*. At the same time, what follows is the structure assumed for the feast day and seasonal liturgies to follow in chapter 5.

Introductory Rites

The introductory rite of the Mass has as its purpose "that the faithful coming together take on the form of a community and prepare themselves to listen to God's word and celebrate the eucharist properly." Therefore every effort should be made to create this disposition in the children and not to jeopardize it by any excess of rites in this part of the Mass.

It is sometimes proper to omit one or other element of the introductory rite or perhaps to expand one of the elements. There should always be at least some introductory element, which is completed by the opening prayer. In choosing individual elements, care should be taken that each one be used from time to time and that none be entirely neglected. (DMC, number 40)

Thus the DMC speaks of the introductory rites. Everything that comes before the first reading from scripture falls into this. Note well the two purposes of the introductory rites:

1. The faithful take on the form of a community.
2. They prepare to listen to God's word and celebrate eucharist.

Those give us the test to apply to these rites as they are prepared for the children's liturgies. Somehow by the time we are addressed by the lector, we are to have gained a sense that what is done here is done by a community. And within that community, we have put aside distractions and preoccupations and are ready to hear God's word, ready then to celebrate the eucharist.

The DMC speaks of the "elements" of the introductory rites. These are things like the opening song, the procession with its possible elements (book, candles, incense), the sign of the cross and the greeting by the presider, any introductory comments, the penitential rite (or the sprinkling rite), the Gloria, the opening prayer ("Let us pray," then silent prayer, then the spoken prayer and its Amen).

The question is: What good use of these elements can we make in our children's liturgies so that introductory rites do their two jobs? That is never a spur-of-the-moment decision by the presider or the musicians. Everything is to be prepared and rehearsed by the ministers so that they can serve the assembly well.

The liturgies suggested in chapter 5 offer a variety of approaches to the introductory rites. The sign of the cross and greeting and opening prayer are constants; they are familiar ground for the assembly at each liturgy. The penitential rite is used only in Lent where it is somewhat extended. The sprinkling rite is used only in Easter. Song is used almost always, though in a variety of ways, for what better way is there to sense that we are here as a community and will act as a community?

The choice of elements is not arbitrary. If these rites are intended to prepare us to hear God's word, then they must prepare us for God's word *in this liturgy*, this Advent liturgy or this Holy Cross liturgy. So they set a tone for what we will hear in the liturgy of the word.

Beginnings are crucial—any place, any time. Those who lead these beginnings of the liturgy must be able to make it all work together the first time. Processions aren't easy things—they have to be practiced. Carrying a book or a candle well isn't easy. Neither is holding the book so that the presider can proclaim the opening prayer. Acolytes are vital to the entrance rites.

So are the people called greeters, ushers or ministers of hospitality. Sometimes they are not needed at a small group's liturgy, but when many different classes come together, they are important. They are especially vital when the format of the day's liturgy suggests that *everyone*, and not just the ministers, be involved in the procession from classroom to church or other worship space. Here we need lively and sensible ushers/guides to get us where we are going.

Just to preside at an entrance rite a person has to: know how to be present in a procession, singing if the assembly is singing; know how to *lead* the sign of the cross; know how to open the arms and look at the assembly and speak the greeting, using the beautiful but formal words of the liturgy that evoke the assembly's response; know how to be brief in any introductory comment, brief but effective for this group of children; know how to invite "Let us pray" and truly mean it, then lead silent prayer (for a long enough time that stillness can come to the room), then speak the practiced words of the opening prayer in such a way that they will catch the attention of a child or an adult.

Being the musician for an entrance rite means having a sense for how music and singing together make us a community, and for the music that can do this in Advent, the music that can do it in Lent. It means bringing that music to the assembly—beforehand in the classroom, then in the liturgy.

All of these ministries are for people who know how important beginnings are, know how to work as a team, know that they are members of the assembly who are charged to help all their brothers and sisters enter into this liturgy.

All who prepare and lead the entrance rites need to remember whose entrance we are talking about here. It is not the entrance of the ministers that is the topic here, but the entrance of the assembly into its liturgy. That's the task.

Liturgy of the Word

Much was said about the liturgy of the word in chapter 2. This and numbers 41–49 of the DMC (see the appendix of this volume) should be reviewed.

Whether there are two or three readings, or only the gospel, and whether the psalm and gospel acclamation are both sung or only one, the liturgy of the word has a structure that is constant: God's word, homily, intercessions.

At its fullest, on a Sunday or Solemnity, the liturgy of the word looks like this (those parts that may be omitted at liturgies with children are placed in brackets):

[Reading and silent reflection]
[Psalm refrain with psalm verse sung or read]
[Reading and silent reflection]
[Sung gospel acclamation and procession]
Gospel with its introduction and conclusion
   Homily [and silent reflection]
[Dismissal of the catechumens]
[Profession of faith]
Intercessions

If there is a general pattern suggested for the liturgies of this book, it would include one reading and the psalm leading to the gospel acclamation and the gospel. For Lent and Eastertime it is suggested that the eucharist be celebrated more often and that the liturgy of the word be quite simple.

The DMC and common sense tell us that the selection and the presentation of the scriptures are both important. Far better that everyone *hear* and be drawn in by a single reader than that many be involved in the reading or dramatizing, but with the assembly left in confusion.

Though the psalm is an option in Masses for children, it should rarely, if ever, be omitted. The psalms are how Christians learn to pray and we have an opportunity to use them in every liturgy. The *Hymnal* includes those psalm refrains that are most likely to be helpful to the seasons and feasts of the school year. Settings for a cantor are available in a separate volume. Note that the psalms need not be restricted to the liturgy of the word; they also make good choices for the communion procession because the assembly has only a refrain to sing and so does not need a book. Likewise, the psalms learned at the eucharist should be used in classroom prayer. The children can discuss the often vivid words of the psalms and find contexts where they are true today. In praying the psalms, we pray as the church and our voices become the voices of people in all situations.

The book of the scriptures is always carried with reverence. This is especially true during the procession that leads to the proclamation of the gospel; it may be honored with incense on great feasts and it is always kissed when the reading of the gospel is completed. The book used at children's Masses, as much as that used at the parish Sunday Mass, should appear worthy of its task.

The DMC notes that:

> With the consent of the pastor or rector of the church, one of the adults may speak to the children after the gospel, especially if the priest finds it difficult to adapt himself to the mentality of children. (DMC, number 24)

Whether the preacher is the presider or another adult, this person has the responsibility to prepare by engaging in reflection on the scriptures and the life of the community. The words will be few. Either directly or indirectly, the good preacher will engage the children in a dialogue. This should ordinarily be followed by some moments of silence.

The outline above suggests that the dismissal of the catechumens takes place after the homily. Catechumens are usually not present at these Masses with children. Some would raise a question here about the children who have not yet received their first communion. In some schools, they do not attend the children's liturgies at all; in others, they are present for the whole liturgy. Yet other parishes have decided that at school Masses these children should be present for the liturgy of the word and then be dismissed much as the catechumens are, to continue elsewhere the conversation about the scriptures and their preparation for first communion. Such a practice could help all to understand that our presence for the liturgy of the eucharist is not a spectator's presence but the activity of a baptized person. Note that it is not simply a matter of who has received communion already. Rather, it is a matter of who has been initiated into full participation in the whole eucharistic action, an action that includes receiving holy communion.

The prayers of intercession conclude the liturgy of the word. The community should become familiar with one or two ways of speaking or singing this litany. It begins with the presider asking all to join in prayer for all our needs. This invitation should be brief; the words are directed to the assembly and not to God. Then the cantor (or another leader if the petitions are not sung) begins the petitions. Except on very rare occasions, the response should remain the same. The most usual forms are: "Lord, have mercy"; "Lord, hear our prayer"; and the Greek "Kyrie eleison." Sometimes a great deal of time is spent in writing long, involved petitions. This is nearly always a mistake. The petitions should be short and direct, always praying for the church, for those in positions of power, for the poor and for the local community. Many things can come under these headings, but no heading should be ignored. Because this is a litany form of prayer, it depends on rather rhythmic movement between the leader and the assembly. The intercessions conclude with the presider gathering them into a brief prayer to which all respond "Amen."

What is important in this part of the liturgy is that the community have an ordered and involving way of doing things, and that both ministers and assembly be at home with that order. This approach sets us free to do well what is the heart of the liturgy: good reading that invites good listening, good homilies, good intercessions. A worthy book, a proper gospel procession, silences at the right time and for a consistent length of time, reflective singing of the psalm and enthusiastic singing of the gospel acclamation, a consistently strong way of doing the intercessions: these give this liturgy to the assembly. The children can be at home here.

The Liturgy of the Eucharist: Preparation of the Altar and the Gifts

Often there are suggestions that various objects be brought forward with the bread and wine: artwork, symbols of the saints, etc. Resist such suggestions. The entrance procession—which can often involve many persons or even the whole assembly—is the time to bring things into the assembly's midst (and the recessional is the time to carry them out). This time is for setting the table. Besides the bread and wine, the only things that should be collected from the assembly now are gifts for the church and the poor. That is the nature of the collection taken up at Sunday Mass. At children's Masses, it is seldom in place to pass the basket, but there are times when gifts for the poor should be brought forward with the bread and wine.

Instrumental music may be played at this time, but usually without singing. We need a quiet moment before we begin the eucharistic prayer.

What is all important is the manner in which the table and gifts are prepared. A good practice is to introduce young children gradually to the objects and furniture of the worship space: what they are, what we do with them, how they are handled. These introductions should convey a true sense of reverence. The difficulty is that this reverence in the adults and in the older children should come from a reverence we foster for everything worthy in God's creation and in the work of human hands. Those with no reverence for the bread of the supper table will be without real reverence for the bread of the eucharistic table. Perhaps, though, we can try to work at both together. The few simple things that we use at liturgy—altar table, candles, cross, book of the scriptures and book of prayers, tablecloth, vesture of the presider, plates and cups, bread and wine—are all to be so made that they call forth our reverence, our sense for God's presence among us. So the first thing is to strive to have worthy furnishings and objects and the second thing is to treat them as such.

All of that becomes visible, tangible, at this moment in the liturgy. Some members of the assembly—chosen and rehearsed beforehand—prepare the table. This can include spreading the cloth, bringing the vessels and the bread and wine. It should be unhurried. The good practice of liturgy is not unraveled by the big things that go wrong occasionally but by these little things when they are done consistently without care or attention.

When the table is ready, the presider comes to it and, with the same reverence shown by the children, fills the cup with wine and a few drops of water and completes the preparation for the eucharistic prayer.

The Liturgy of the Eucharist: The Eucharistic Prayer

The DMC speaks with some urgency about the place of the eucharistic prayer:

> The eucharistic prayer is of the greatest importance in the eucharist celebrated with children because it is the high point of the entire celebration. Much depends upon the manner in which the priest proclaims this prayer and in which the children take part by listening and making their acclamations.
>
> The disposition of mind required for this central part of the celebration, the calm and reverence with which everything is done, should make the children as attentive as possible. They should be attentive to the real presence of Christ on the altar under the species of bread and wine, to his offering, to the thanksgiving through him and with him and in him, and to the offering of the church which is made during the prayer and by which the faithful offer themselves and their lives with Christ to the eternal Father in the Holy Spirit. (DMC, number 52)

We have had much difficulty, since the reform of the liturgy, in doing the eucharistic prayer in the manner described here. It simply has not been experienced by adults or by children as the high point of the whole liturgy. Perhaps those who prepare the liturgy—presiders and cantors especially—need to consider the qualities enumerated in the DMC:

- the manner in which the priest proclaims the prayer
- the manner in which the children take part by listening and making their acclamations
- the disposition of mind
- the calm and reverence with which everything is done
- attention to the real presence of Christ, to the thanksgiving, to the offering of the church and of ourselves

The eucharistic prayer is to be experienced time after time as the high point of our participation. That is achieved through the sort of leadership described in the qualities listed above and through a form of the eucharistic prayer that allows for strong acclamation by the whole assembly. This should begin with the responses in the dialogue: "And also with you," "We lift them up to the Lord," "It is right to give him thanks and praise." It should continue through the Sanctus and the one or several other acclamations within the eucharistic prayer. It should climax with the singing of the great Amen.

The challenge is to find a way of doing this. It requires good, familiar, singable music for the acclamations. It requires a presider who knows that this is not simply a long monologue but a prayer proclaimed by one person and acclaimed several or many times by all present. That relationship, that understanding is crucial. Presiders often need help in achieving this, including thoughtful evaluation from others. Those in charge of music need a sense for how the music is to serve the assembly here. Only a limited repertory is necessary or desirable. Presider and musician together need a practiced sense of timing so that the prayer can achieve a naturalness that comes only from careful and patient work.

In the first liturgies of each school year, it may be best to begin with one of the six eucharistic prayers in normal use on Sundays (called eucharistic prayers 1 through 4 and the two eucharistic prayers for Masses of reconciliation). Perhaps with Advent or Lent, when the eucharist is celebrated more frequently and there has been time for practice, the eucharistic prayers for Masses with children can be used. The first of these three eucharistic prayers uses parts of the Sanctus for additional acclamations in the first part of the prayer. The second uses additional acclamations throughout the prayer and, if done properly, is by far the strongest of the three. The third uses an acclamation several times in the last part of the prayer. The *Hymnal* provides two settings for the acclamations of the second eucharistic prayer. Acclamations, of course, are by their nature something to know by heart. The *Hymnal* is used for learning them, but not at the liturgy itself.

In some places it is customary for the children to stand close to the table during the eucharistic prayer. This should be done only when everyone, adults included, can come around the table. Sometimes the numbers are too large for this to work well. Such a practice requires that all—presider and assembly—know what they are doing so that they can join in this prayer with greater attention, not less, because of their nearness to one another. It is not a show by the presider for the children, nor a cute entertainment the children provide for adults in the background. It is this assembly at the most intense moment of its liturgy.

The Liturgy of the Eucharist: The Communion Rite

The communion rite will be strongest when it follows the same order each time. This means that the order itself has been carefully prepared. The elements are these:

Lord's Prayer
[Peace greeting]
Breaking of the bread
Invitation to communion
Communion procession and song
Silence [song of praise]
Prayer after communion

Note that the peace greeting is in brackets. The DMC (number 53) does not mention it as one of the required elements for Masses with children (though it is mentioned earlier in number 23). This is probably because the peace greeting is always an option, even at the Sunday Mass. In Masses with children, it requires a careful judgment as to whether or not it is appropriate. Some have placed it elsewhere (at the beginning or the ending of the liturgy). Careful consideration is needed.

Apart from this question, the structure is very simple and very important. All recite or sing the Lord's Prayer together. Then (after the peace greeting if it is given here) the presider lifts up the bread and begins to break it for communion as the assembly sings the Lamb of God. This is a litany and should last as long as it takes for the presider and communion ministers to prepare the bread and cups for communion. When this is done, the litany concludes ("Grant us peace"), and the presider invites all to the table: "This is the Lamb of God . . ." The presider takes communion and at once the communion of the assembly begins (leaving the ministers to receive after everyone else). If all are gathered around the altar, the ministers (adults from the school or parish community) take appointed positions so that the children can approach them and then return to their places. If all have not gathered around the altar, then student ushers can help to direct the procession.

The communion song begins immediately after the invitation to communion. This music is such that it can be sung without a book: chants in the Taizé style, psalm refrains, compositions in the style of "Gift of finest wheat." All of these leave the "one time" words to a cantor and give the people the repeatable text. Note that the words sung need not have any immediate reference to holy communion, but neither should they be directly about something different. Thus Psalm 114 with the refrain "God has freed us and redeemed us" is a good choice for a communion song as is "Jesu, Jesu," even though neither one has explicit reference to the communion rite. "O come, O come, Emmanuel," even though it has a refrain, might be less desirable as a communion song.

What matters greatly is that the manner of the procession and the song come together to be an expression of this holy communion that we are. The ministers of communion have their part in this also. Their way of standing, speaking and giving bread and cup are important in conveying that "body of Christ" and "blood of Christ" are our name.

The bread that is used should be such that it fulfills the requirement that it have the appearance of food. Such bread can be purchased from some suppliers; it can also be baked locally from recipes that use only wheat flour and water. All of the bread for holy communion at a given liturgy is to be brought forward and consecrated at that liturgy. These are norms of the Roman rite.

After communion the vessels are placed on a table to one side for purifying after Mass. The presider and other ministers take their places so that there may be a time of quiet reflection. A song of praise is also possible at this time, but seldom necessary. After the silence, the presider and all stand for the prayer after communion.

Of all the parts of the Mass, the communion rite is the one in which the assembly takes a full and constant part—from the Lord's Prayer through the peace greeting and the Lamb of God (to accompany the breaking of the bread) to the communion itself and the silence together afterwards. The consistent way in which the community does this rite will form and reform the participants who are themselves the body of Christ. As the DMC says, "If [children] are formed by conscious and active participation in the eucharistic sacrifice and meal, they should learn day by day, at home and away from home, to proclaim Christ to others among their family and among their peers, by living the faith, which expresses itself through love" (DMC, number 55).

Concluding Rite

The presider now greets the assembly and speaks the blessing. The latter may be the brief form, though on great feasts it can take the more solemn form with several responses of Amen.

The presider then says the words of dismissal and the assembly responds "Thanks be to God." Often a song is the best conclusion (although this is not a part of the the Roman rite), sometimes with a procession of the ministers, sometimes with a procession by everyone if some activity or social time is to follow, and sometimes without any procession as presider and assembly simply stay and sing together.

PART TWO

The Liturgies

In this chapter suggestions are offered for the principal eucharistic liturgies and other prayer services of the school year. Those using this material should be familiar with all that has been said in earlier chapters, especially chapter 4, and should make constant use of the "Index of Music" found in the Appendix. Page references in this index and in the references below are to pages in the *Hymnal for Catholic Students*.

Prayer Service to Begin the School Year

The eucharistic liturgy for the feast of the Holy Cross or for the feast day of Michael, Gabriel and Raphael is suggested as the entrance into the school year. In many places, a gathering on the first or second day of school will also be customary. This is often too soon for there to be a full celebration of the eucharist (with musicians, lectors and others prepared for their tasks), but a very simple liturgy to bless and begin the school year could take place. This might be in each classroom, or within age groups, or for the whole school (in which case administrators and helpers of all kinds would be present also).

Such a service helps to welcome new members of the school community: the youngest students, those who have transferred, new faculty and staff. The service should not be confused with an orientation (that is, it isn't for introductions as such, let alone discussing responsibilities or rules), but should manifest the hospitality of the community. In some places, older students will have been assigned to a new student. These pairs might be together for this introductory prayer service.

The presider at this service could be the pastor or, because it is not a eucharist, it could be the principal.

The order of service could be adapted from the prayers for the beginning or ending of the day or could be a liturgy of the word in this form:

Song (e.g., "Gather us in" from page 124, "This little light of mine" from page 196)

Sign of the cross, greeting, prayer

Scripture reading (e.g., Luke 8:16–18 about the lamp on a lampstand)

Homily (rather than many comments here and there in the liturgy, the presider should use this one moment in the liturgy to speak of welcome, of the school, of the new year beginning, and all this in light of the scripture just proclaimed)

Intercessions for the church, the world, the poor, the parish, the school and all its many members

Lord's Prayer

Blessing

Song (repeat some verses of the opening song)

September 14, The Holy Cross

BACKGROUND

This is an old feast related to the discovery of the true cross. By the fourth century, the cross had become for Christians a symbol of Christ's triumph. In this single image—the sign of the cross—they found the whole paschal mystery: "Dying, he destroyed our death; rising, he restored our life." As Christianity spread, the cross was to be found in places of worship, in homes, in burial places. In a gesture made with the hand or in lines carved into stone or in wood or metal forms, the cross has been for us the meeting of earth and heaven, God and humankind, God's mercy and our offense.

This feast is an appropriate occasion to begin the eucharistic celebrations of the school year. It comes as the fall equinox approaches so that we raise the cross against the gathering darkness. Each year this could be the first gathering of the entire school. At it, children and teachers would celebrate this very tangible manifestation of what binds them to one another as people baptized into Christ's death. This feast is an autumn reminder of the mysteries we celebrate fully in spring, especially at the Easter Vigil. In relation to the school year, the feast on September 14 allows us to proclaim: "We begin our work, our year together, by placing ourselves and this school community under the sign of the cross."

Note that when this liturgy is the first eucharist of the school year, the liturgy is still about the holy cross. It does not become a liturgy about the beginning of the school year. Rather, because it is about the holy cross, it can say a good deal about the school community that gathers and celebrates.

Do not overuse the sign of the cross at this or any other liturgy. Usually only a single cross is present at the place where the liturgy is celebrated. Avoid making the sign of the cross at any extra places in the liturgy (e.g., before or after the homily) and just do it well at the ordinary times when it is called for.

CLASSROOM PREPARATION

Teachers and children alike should attend to the place of the cross in their lives. At baptism, the sign of the cross is traced on the infant's or adult's forehead as the presider says: "I claim you for Christ our Savior by the sign of his cross." Parents and godparents and other witnesses are then invited to follow the presider's lead and to trace the cross again and again on the child's forehead. Sometimes this gesture will be a familiar way for the parent to bless the young child at night. The sign of the cross may be present in the home—made together at the dinner table or with night prayers and present also in a cross hung on the wall—or it may be absent. Teachers should not presume too much or too little here, but they should introduce the children to what is appropriate and to the way the cross is used not only in baptism but the anointing of the sick and at the time of death and burial.

At all levels of the school, look at the ways the sign of the cross is made during the liturgy and practice these. Talk about the difference between the sign of the cross made at the very beginning of the liturgy and the cross made before the gospel. How is the sign of the cross made over the bread and wine during the eucharistic prayer? How is it made at the final blessing? Actual practice is best.

The refrain of the spirited hymn, "Lift high the cross," should be introduced and practiced in every classroom as the liturgy approaches.

Primary

The simplest introduction to signs might come through in: "When you see the Golden Arches, what does that tell you?" Photos or other images for Brownies or Cub Scouts can be used, the school logo or team insignia also. Go to the church to see and touch the cross that is used to lead the procession at Sunday liturgy. In some cases, this will be a crucifix (the cross with the image of Jesus on it). Even so, stress the cross so that the children see what is common between this image and the image they trace on themselves to begin the day or the liturgy. While in church, talk about the cross that is made on the infant or the adult in preparation for baptism. Visit the baptismal font. Go to the holy water font by the door and practice making the sign of the cross with blessed water: How is this to remind us that we are baptized? A bright cross might be made for the bulletin board in the classroom and the children could come forward to put their names on the cross saying, "I belong to Jesus."

Intermediate

Focus on symbols of victory: a crown, a medal, a trophy. The cross is also a sign of victory. The children can bring the processional cross for the liturgy to the classroom and decorate it for the liturgy. Make tissue paper flowers to attach, or beautiful ribbons, or "jewels" made from bright paper and glitter. Have the students gather around the completed cross and recall that to be a "victor" implies discipline and struggle. Against what did Jesus struggle? Talk about the Good Friday liturgy and how the cross is brought in and venerated. Bring the book that has the words that are sung.

When it is possible for the liturgy itself to begin with a procession from the school classrooms, these students might be the leaders of the procession. A few of the students could work with the adult cantor so that they can be leaders for the hymn, "Lift high the cross." Then, with students (who have practiced carrying the cross high with great dignity) carrying the cross, they can go from classroom to classroom inviting all to join in procession to the church or other area for the liturgy. At each classroom, a selected student announces: "Jesus is victorious! Come and follow the cross!"

Junior high

With the students, explore how the cross has been depicted in art, poetry and hymns. Or look into the way that the sign of the cross is used in the celebration of each of the sacraments.

With this liturgy and others that take place near the beginning of the school year, it is best if these older students take all the leadership roles in the liturgy itself. The importance of their example as followers of Jesus should be stressed: in school and out. All the necessary help should be given so that those chosen can serve well as acolytes, greeters and perhaps readers.

Junior high students could also make nametags for all members of the student body. More particularly and personally, each student could be asked to accompany a new student from the primary grades to the liturgy and to review with that child the proper way to make the sign of the cross.

LITURGY PREPARATION

Only one cross should be used, not many. Normally this will be the processional cross as used each Sunday. In the procession it can be adorned as noted above, and it can be honored by those who carry candles and walk beside it and by a pot of fragrant incense placed near it (reminding us of the bittersweetness of the cross).

Whether or not the liturgy begins with the procession described above, the beginning will be the singing of "Lift high the cross." The students might learn only the refrain; the verses can be sung by a cantor or by a small group of students who have prepared the music. The refrain is strong and should become an important part of the school repertory, a rousing piece that can be anticipated year after year to begin this first eucharistic liturgy.

After the hymn, the presider introduces the sign of the cross with a few prepared words that invite the children to make the gesture thoughtfully and carefully. For example:

> As we gather on this feast of the Holy Cross, we begin our celebration with a gesture that we make every day. With care and with love, let us begin—In the name of the Father, and of the Son, and of the Holy Spirit.

Make the sign of the cross slowly and deliberately—as at every liturgy.

After the sign of the cross, invite, "Let us pray," and pause for silence and stillness. Then read the opening prayer with care that it be understood by the children.

Use only the first reading (Numbers 21:4–9) and the gospel. The vivid description of the grumbling people lends itself to some pantomime or dramatization if this can be done well. The processional cross might be used as the bronze serpent. After a period of silence, move to the gospel with a procession led, for this once, by the cross. The presider follows, holding high the gospel book and accompanied by two or more children carrying candles and perhaps incense. Accompany the procession with a rousing alleluia (perhaps the Celtic alleluia, *Hymnal*, page 75, which would otherwise be used only in Eastertime—thus giving this appropriate feast an echo of the Easter season that was being celebrated as the previous school year concluded). Deliberate care should be taken with the sign of the cross at the announcement of the gospel.

If gestures have been made carefully, the homily is easy. Practicing the sign of the cross could be part of it, along with reflection on the various sets of words (and sometimes silence) with which we accompany the cross. Some of the older children might be asked (and prepared beforehand) to demonstrate how we can bless one another with the sign of the cross made on the forehead. Suggest to the children how they can bless their parents and little brothers and sisters. Talk about how the beginning and ending of life and the beginning and ending of each day is to be marked with the sign of the cross. Talk about the beginning of the school year, and the coming change in the seasons marking an end to the warmth and growth of summer and its long days. The church places the cross here at this time of transition. Words and images from "Lift high the cross" should be studied and incorporated into the homily.

The general intercessions are always prepared according to the order of prayer for the church, for those in positions of authority in the world, for the needs of the world and of the poor, for the local community. Make these specific to the feast by praying that the cross may offer protection against war and hunger, that it might bring healing to those in pain and blessing to all who begin this school year.

The table is then simply prepared and the bread and wine brought forward. Use the preface for the Holy Cross. Perhaps the use of the special eucharistic prayers for Masses with children should be delayed until there has been more time to prepare the pattern of proclamation and acclamation needed in two of these prayers. The musical setting chosen for the acclamations today should be the simplest in the repertory and should be used through the fall until another is mastered. The communion refrain can also be kept the same for several liturgies during this first part of the year. "Eat this bread" is one possibility; see the index for other suggestions.

Take care again at the final blessing with the sign of the cross. The dismissal could be: "Made strong with the cross, protected by Christ's cross, go forth to love and serve the Lord." Sing the remaining stanzas of "Lift high the cross" as the closing hymn and let all process singing from the worship space.

September 29: Michael, Gabriel, Raphael

BACKGROUND
This feast is also an excellent choice for the initial eucharist of the school year. Like the Holy Cross, it is a feast especially placed to stand at the turn of the seasons. Originally, the church celebrated Michael, the great protector, here, but now adds those angels whose stories tell of their being messengers and healers.

Review how the angels are present throughout our scriptures. They eat with Abraham and hear Sarah laughing, they wrestle with

Jacob, they protect and guide Tobiah, they singe Isaiah's tongue and announce the good news to Zachary and Mary and Joseph, they battle the forces of Satan. Scripture and Catholic tradition have given a significant place to angels: messengers and guardians, choirs and armies. In an age when people often feel isolated, the idea of someone walking with us, caring for us, protecting us and bringing us the message of God's love is good news indeed. We celebrate the angels as messengers of God's love and as companions on our journey.

CLASSROOM PREPARATION

On all levels, the preparation should involve review of some of the many scripture stories that involve the angels (use a concordance and teach at least the older students what a concordance to the Bible is and how it works). And it should include a review or introduction to the two angel songs we use at the liturgy, the Gloria (find the first words in Luke's gospel) and the Sanctus (find the "Holy holy holy" in Isaiah). Preparation for the liturgy would include practice in singing the appropriate version of the Gloria or Sanctus or the hymn "Holy holy holy" (page 132) if that is to be sung.

In all the stories and catechesis, avoid the temptation to use male pronouns for the angels, even for these three whose names are male names in English. Angels, like God, have no sex in Catholic tradition, but with both angels and God we have the unfortunate habit of speaking with male pronouns. Work against this.

Be sure to prepare to mark the name's day of any children with angels as their patrons: Michael and Michel, Gabriel and Gabriela, Rafael and Raphael, Angela and Angelo. Learn the meaning of these Hebrew names. "Michael," for example, is a battle cry of a name; it means, "Who is like God?" (It is a good idea to find a name's day for every child early in the school year, to identify these on the calendar and to observe these days with a special intercession at Morning Prayer.)

Primary

Use scripture stories of Gabriel as messenger, Raphael as healer, Michael as warrior. Explore the children's ideas of what an angel can do and what their angels might be like. Learn the prayer:

> Angel sent by God to guide me,
> be my light and walk beside me;
> be my guardian and protect me;
> on the paths of life direct me.

This is simply a more contemporary reading of the "Angel of God" prayer. It will be found in the "Prayers" section of the *Hymnal*. Another prayer will be familiar to many adults and could well be taught to children as a night prayer:

> Now I lay me down to sleep,
> I pray the Lord my soul to keep.
> Four corners to my bed,
> Four angels there aspread:
> Two to foot and two to head,
> And four to carry me when I'm dead.
> If any danger come to me,
> Sweet Jesus Christ deliver me.
> And if I die before I wake,
> I pray the Lord my soul to take.

If the students are asked to imagine and draw angels, don't limit them to your own images. Their work might be placed in various locations around the school in the days before the liturgy.

Intermediate

In small groups the students could find, read and plan how they would act out various angel stories from scripture. Then they might act these out for one another and make a list of all the things angels do. Strive for good breadth in the qualities: strength as well as tenderness, boldness as well as obedience. Perhaps these students could make posters to help the new school year along: "Be an angel! Walk someone home from school today." "Be an angel! Watch out for younger children on the playground." Have them reflect on why so much Christian art has shown angels with wings.

Junior high

Have the students find the angels in art. Look especially around the church itself (some will turn up many surprises in older buildings). Should some of these angels on the inside or outside of the church be given ribbons or other decoration to call attention to them on the feast day? Study the scripture stories also and discuss how these oldest students can be companions, protectors and messengers. How have they experienced these gifts in others when they were younger? Be concrete in stories and examples: We can be companions by listening to classmates who are upset, by inviting people into our games and activities. We can be protectors by not listening to or spreading stories that hurt people. Could they write a thank-you to someone who has been an "angel" in their lives?

LITURGY PREPARATION

The liturgy might begin with a preparatory reading by a good storyteller (who may even have memorized the text) of Isaiah 6:1–4. This can be followed immediately by an opening hymn (e.g., "Holy holy holy" from page 132 or "We see the Lord" from page 202; both pick up on the Isaiah text). Instead of a procession, the ministers can be in place and singing with the assembly, perhaps also adding incense to a pot of hot coals placed in the midst of the space. (This incense might also be placed in front of a fine icon of an angel or a good picture that is well mounted for exhibiting in this way.)

The presider should beware of the temptation to break the spirit of this gathering with an overly casual greeting ("Hi, boys and girls"). Informality belongs earlier, welcoming the students as they come from their classrooms. Here, make the sign of the cross carefully and deliberately. Greet the students and call attention to any angels the church displays (neglected the rest of the year) or, lacking these, to the angel in the icon in front of which the incense is burning. Be aware that incense has many "meanings," including the rising of our prayers and the "cloud" of God's presence.

In general it will be best to be simple and move to the "Let us pray," the silence and the opening prayer. However, depending on the preparation for this liturgy, it may be good to recite the Confiteor (". . . all the angels and saints . . .") or to sing the Gloria (with its opening words from the angels' song to the shepherds).

Use either (but not both) of the two readings provided for this day. If the first is chosen, a good storyteller could memorize the text and tell it without the book. The psalm refrain (from Psalm 138, page 65, "In the sight of the angels I will sing your praises, Lord") should be taught in the days before and sung now. Psalm verses can be sung by a cantor or read by a reader. After the psalm, allow some silent time before the gospel procession and its acclamation. The homily can simply direct the children to the sights, sounds (words of songs and of scriptures) and smells (incense). Like the angels, we are to be companions, protectors of one another, bearers of good news. These notions should also shape the writing of the intercessions.

The eucharistic prayer and acclamations should be done as noted on the feast of the Holy Cross. The Sanctus should have special significance today, but let this speak for itself without commentary. During it, more incense could be placed on the coals. Use the same communion refrain as for the Holy Cross.

Dismiss the assembly with an echo of the homily, "Go as messengers of the good news to love and serve the Lord." Sing more of the opening hymn or "Ye watchers and ye holy ones" (page 210).

October 4: Saint Francis of Assisi

BACKGROUND

The well-loved but not-so-imitated Francis lived in the 13th century in a little town a few hours from Rome. He was raised in riches, but eventually heard the gospel very clearly and decided he needed to be free of possessions to serve God by serving the poor. Among other things, Christians have learned from Francis about the stewardship of creation (read about the sixth day of creation in Genesis 1) and about living in peace together. Teachers should take time to learn much about Francis; a book entitled *Francis* (New York: Collier) would be one possible classroom resource.

CLASSROOM PREPARATION

The many stories and legends surrounding Francis are engrossing preparation for all age levels. These stories should be shared with the children as appropriate. This will be the basic preparation for the liturgy each year. A good deal of Francis' life is summed up in his Canticle of the Sun in which he addresses the sun as "Brother" and the moon as "Sister," and so on through creation. Each year the students could learn a line or two of this prayer to use at appropriate times. And each year they would practice also the song which is based on Francis' poem, "All creatures of our God and King."

If a field trip to the zoo or to a natural history museum is in order at any time during the year, it might be planned near the feast of Francis.

Primary

Use a good children's Bible to explore the Genesis story of creation. Make a mural and be sure that the refrain, "God saw how good it was," comes through in both story and picture. Practice the hymn, "All creatures of our God and King" (page 100), discussing how it comes from a wonderful prayer Francis made up. The children may want to choose roles and take the part of the various creatures as the song is sung: Someone is the sun, someone the moon, others the fire, the water, the wind and so on. In such a "good" creation, what is our task? How did Francis think about this?

Intermediate

Read or tell the story of Francis and the wolf of Gubbio. Invite the children to share stories and pictures of people who have this kind of love for God's creatures. If the feast of Francis is to include the blessing of an animal to represent all the pets of the children, the intermediate children might be in charge of this each year. (In some places, the blessing should be parishwide. The blessing for the animals can be found in *Catholic Household Blessings and Prayers*.) In discussions and other stories, the example of Francis as one who loved and cared for all creatures can be applied to contemporaries and to the children themselves. Who are the peacemakers today? Have some of them been a bit like Francis?

Junior high

Discuss the life of Francis and learn the prayer that is often called "The Prayer of Saint Francis" (even though it was written much later). Discuss each line. Where is there hatred and how could someone bring love? Where is there injury in our homes, classroom, community, city, world? How can we show pardon? Pairs or teams of students might be assigned to read or interview outside the classroom and bring back the thoughts of others on such questions.

LITURGY PREPARATION

The season is harvesttime and that goes well with Francis and his care of the earth and of the poor. Squash, pumpkins, corn, wheat and other gifts can fill baskets by the entrance into the worship space and near altar and ambo. These are not for today only but are for the late autumn feasts also.

The procession might be one to involve everyone, with many carrying the fruits of the earth. The verses of "All creatures of our God and King" can be sung by cantor and a small group of children while all are well prepared from classroom use to come in on the refrain, the alleluias that punctuate each verse of this wonderful song. The rite can climax with the sign of the cross, simple greeting and opening prayer.

The option of choosing more appropriate scriptures might be exercised by turning to the creation story in Genesis 1, perhaps using 1:1, 26–31 if a shorter reading seems best. Sing Psalm 104 with its refrain asking God to renew the face of the earth. After some silence, begin the gospel procession and its acclamation. The alleluia here can be taken right from "All creatures." An appropriate gospel text is Matthew 25:14–23, the parable of the talents. The homily can be about Francis and what he has to show the world and about the people today who have found him a good teacher. The intercessions need to express concerns that embrace the health of the earth and its creatures.

If the liturgy includes the blessing of an animal "representative," the blessing would follow a very short homily and the liturgy would conclude with a blessing of the children. In the blessing of the animals, be sure that the children are themselves asked to join in giving this blessing.

Acclamations and communion refrains established in the earlier liturgies should be repeated in today's eucharistic prayer.

Repeated verses of "All creatures" are appropriate as a closing song as is the song "Sing out, earth and skies" (also well-suited to using a cantor with the students singing only the refrain).

November 1: All Saints

BACKGROUND

November, the end of harvest and the beginning of the earth's winter sleep, has been a time to remember the dead. In this, the church simply followed the lead of the peoples who lived in the northern lands. The feasts we keep in early November have ancient roots. Like every other people, Christians need and want to remember their dead, the ancestors, and to pray for them and with them. All around us is a battle raging: cold against warmth, light against dark, life against death. What we learn, perhaps, is that cold and dark and death are also God's creatures (that was something Francis of Assisi knew well). Halloween, All Saints Day, All Souls Day and the whole month of November manifest different dimensions of what we like to call the communion of saints. These are days when the Sunday readings bring us to the end of Matthew or Mark or Luke and thus to stories of the judgment times. These days then turn into Advent when the whole liturgy has us looking toward the Lord's return.

In our prayer and in the songs and stories of these days, we grow each year a little nearer to our own death, a little more ready to pray "Maranatha," "Come, Lord Jesus." We do this by growing in understanding and in a living sense for what it is we are saying in the Creed when we say things about how we "look for the resurrection of the dead and the life of the world to come" (or, in the Apostles Creed, that we believe in "the communion of saints, the forgiveness of sins, the resurrection of the body, and the life everlasting"). These are not simply items to be studied when they come up in religion class, they are part of the Catholic way of life that we encounter especially in November.

All Saints Day is a Holy Day. This may mean that children will join other parishioners for the liturgy. Hospitality—from both sides—should be considered and prepared. Neither group should feel like spectators at the other group's liturgy.

CLASSROOM PREPARATION

The preparation for the liturgy and the follow-up during the rest of November (leading on to Thanksgiving and to Advent also) involve careful plans for marking in story, song, art and discussion the mysteries that these days bring into focus: the communion of saints, the time of fulfillment, death itself. A parish should see itself as involved in this celebration with all its parishioners and the school taking its appropriate part.

This may well involve going with the children to visit a cemetery, discussing the deaths of relatives, learning how the church prays with the dying and then with mourners and how we keep vigil and celebrate the funeral rites of the dead. It would also involve having the children explore the litany of the church's saints, taking care to point out and study those who have most to offer us. All of this can be quite demanding, but (as with much that is suggested here) the only truly helpful approach is to let each year build on the last, establishing good practices and coming back to them year after year.

At every level, the stories of saints past (including the saints for whom the children are named) should lead to stories of holy people in our own times: those known widely and those known locally. And this in turn leads to looking at all the ways we recognize holiness (beatitudes and commandments and the judgment story of Matthew 25 would be the background for this), and the ways we ourselves are to be part of this communion of saints.

It might become part of the tradition for the children to come for this liturgy in their Halloween costumes, but many factors will go into this decision. Contrary to the ways of the commercial culture, Halloween customs are really All Saints Day and All Souls Day customs. They are part of the "eve" of the festival and of the days themselves. Trick-or-treat is door-to-door hospitality. The jack-o'-lantern is a welcoming light to guide us home. Masks and merriment and the edibles (it's harvest time) are all signs of God's reign, a place where rag-tag children remove their masks and we see who they truly are, the saints of God.

The preparation for this liturgy could be an opportunity to foster relationships between primary and junior high students. The latter could research and tell the stories of their own patron saints or favorite saints. They could also find out the stories of a younger student's patron saint or favorite saint. Then, working one-on-one, the junior high students would tell the stories and help the younger students begin a storybook about the saints. These partners might then attend the liturgy together.

Intermediate

Besides exploring the stories of saints (and perhaps also of ancestors or relations for whom they were named) and some of the other activities mentioned above, these students might take charge of preparing the room for the liturgy and of the school itself for November. Honoring images and pictures and icons of the saints could be part of this, but so could pumpkins and jack-o'-lanterns. Some of the students may come from ethnic traditions that have very visual ways of keeping the month of November (for example, the Mexican shrines).

Liturgy Preparation

The litany of the saints can provide the gathering song for this day and a part of morning prayer for all November. The musical setting could be the traditional one or one that is more contemporary (both found in the Accompaniment Edition for the *Hymnal*). A litany goes well with a procession either of the ministers or of everyone from the classrooms or the gathering place into the church. In preparing the litany, go through the names of the students and include as many of their patrons as possible. A cantor can lead the litany. The pace should be fairly rapid so that the refrain, "Pray for us," becomes like a mantra. The sign of the cross, greeting and opening prayer then conclude the introductory rites.

Choose either the first or second reading from the lectionary and let it be followed with silence. Then the alleluia and gospel procession lead to the vigorous proclamation of the beatitudes. In the homily, talk about the ordinariness of saints. Saints are among us. We can all be saintly. Call this assembly "the saints," as the early church did. The saints were real, not phony, not pretenders. That's the way for us, too.

The all-embracing concerns of the saints should come across in the general intercessions.

In the liturgy of the eucharist continue the format and acclamations from earlier liturgies. By now, these should have taken strong root in the assembly. The pace and sounds and gestures of this whole rite must come to belong to the children and that takes both careful leadership and repetition.

"Go in peace, all you saints, to love and serve the Lord and one another," might be the dismissal. A good strong hymn is needed then, such as "When the saints go marching in" (not in the *Hymnal* because neither words nor music will be needed once the song has been learned) or "Sing with all the saints in glory" (page 184) or "What wondrous love is this" (page 208)—a song that *sounds* like November.

Prayer Service for November: All Souls Day

On November 2 or on some other day of this month and season when Catholics are especially aware of the communion of saints, a prayer service or a Mass for the dead ought to be celebrated with the children. This might well be done with individual classes or with several classes together rather than with the whole school. This allows for a more reflective character to the liturgy.

This liturgy is one part of the practices that mark each autumn in the parish. In the keeping of the feast of All Saints, in the presence of a large and beautiful book in which the names of the dead may be written, in visits to cemeteries, in the Sunday and weekday lectionaries for these last weeks of the church year—in all such ways children and adults become aware of how, as Catholics, they are to remember and pray for the dead. (See the background notes above under "November 1: All Saints.")

In preparation for this liturgy, the children might bring lists of their own relatives who have died, adding names of others from the community and other deceased persons for whom the children want to pray (and this can include well-known persons of the distant past or the very recent past). Read and reflect in the classroom on some of the many passages from scripture that are given in the lectionary under "Masses for the Dead." The Order of Christian Funerals also contains these scripture texts along with many prayers that can be used during November. The Index of Music in this book, under "Times of Mourning," lists appropriate songs and psalms. From these elements, the liturgy (whether a Mass or prayer service following the order of the liturgy of the word) can be prepared.

Certain prayers (for example, "Eternal rest grant unto them, O Lord, and let perpetual light shine upon them") should be used daily during this season, becoming part of the basic Catholic vocabulary of prayer. Remembrance of and prayer for the dead at night prayer is part of Catholic tradition. This accompanies prayers ("Now I lay me down to sleep," "Hail, holy queen") in which we daily face our own death. All of this should be discussed each November.

Thanksgiving Prayer Service

BACKGROUND

The school liturgy should not duplicate the parish's Thanksgiving Day service or eucharist. If anything, it should extend an invitation to the students and their families to gather for the liturgy on Thanksgiving Day. Usually the school service would be the last part of the school day on the day before Thanksgiving. It is a simple prayer service.

CLASSROOM PREPARATION

There will usually be some special preparation for Thanksgiving Day and this should also prepare for the liturgy. Younger children can talk about family plans for Thanksgiving Day and list the people who will be together, telling something about each one for whom they are thankful. Older students might write a few lines to be part of the blessing of the table on Thanksgiving Day.

In preparing for Thanksgiving there is an important line between the "thank-you-I'm-not-like-the-rest-of-the-world" approach and a genuine thankfulness. Much of the public rhetoric of the day seems to make power and wealth in a nation the proof of God's blessing. A very different approach emerges from the gospel and from such documents as the United States bishops' pastoral letter, *Economic Justice for All*. Teachers and students alike should work toward a true spirit of thanksgiving for all that is good, a spirit that will be recognized in generosity and in zeal for justice.

Part of the preparation might be gathering specific things that are needed either locally (in a service providing meals for the homeless or food for the poor) or in other cities or countries. These would be gathered in the classrooms and brought to the liturgy before distribution. With the older children especially, these should be their own gifts and not only those provided by parents.

Catholic Household Blessings and Prayers (pages 186–88) suggests that the three days leading up to Thanksgiving may be good choices for annual "ember days," days of penance and charity. This binds our gratitude to our awareness of others' needs. The school may wish to explore what ember days would mean in terms of special prayers and practices—especially any food or clothing collections.

LITURGY PREPARATION

The liturgy is structured as a liturgy of the word. Among the songs appropriate for beginning and ending are: "For the beauty of the earth" (page 120), "All things bright and beautiful" (page 104), "All creatures of our God and King" (page 100), "Come, ye thankful people, come" (page 116).

After the sign of the cross, greeting and opening prayer, the scripture might be the story of the ten lepers (Luke 17:11–19). This could be done with mime or drama. The homilist has the task of making connections to daily life and certainly to the way Catholics gather up their daily life in eucharist on Sundays. "Eucharist" comes from words that have to do with giving thanks. We are invited each Sunday, "Let us give thanks to the Lord our God," and that is what we do.

The intercession might be sung as a litany with many briefly stated intentions. Pray for all the peoples that make up this nation, for justice in our doings, for a spirit of sharing in our relation to all other peoples. Pray for inspiration, courage, and for humility (not one of our national virtues). Pray especially for the descendants of those who inhabited this land first, the native Americans whose cry for justice is still not heard by many. Remember that these are intercessions, not a litany of thanks (a litany of thanks will come best through the hymns and other prayers).

After the Lord's Prayer and blessing, conclude with a rousing song such as "Now thank we all our God" (page 158), "Let all things now living" (page 150), or simply "Praise God from whom all blessings flow" (page 173).

Advent Liturgy

BACKGROUND

The season that begins four Sundays before Christmas has two movements: Advent itself and then Christmastime. The two are always understood and celebrated together. This is especially difficult when the surrounding culture has a very loud shopping season going on. It seems that everything conspires to do away with the keeping of Advent. Even in the school, Christmas decor, pageants, parties and gifts show us unwilling to participate in Advent's darkness and quiet and waiting. Advent is never going to be a matter just of calling some ritual our "Advent prayer service" or our "Advent Mass." Advent is a place where the church is dwelling for these weeks. It is kept in prayer services and at Mass, but only if it is kept in a hundred other ways. As with so many things, we must be convinced that the good to be accomplished is worth the effort. What good would make it worth our while to keep Advent in the school with no Christmas decorations and no carols and no parties and no gifts—until it is Christmas? Advent has this good, a good that can bring a Christmas season that can be a true season, lasting until Epiphany and beyond. Everything that is happening inside children during these days—the *expectation* of Christmas and its gifts and festivity as well as the eagerness to be generous in giving to others—can take root and flourish in a well-kept Advent. School and parish together can begin to uncover some of this, but neither will do so alone. It is the larger community, the parish, that keeps Advent and keeps the Christmas season. The school can be only an extension of this.

Advent's character is caught in its color, in the sound of its songs, in its scripture stories and psalms. It flows out of the remembering of November and becomes a sort of longing, a sense of what is missing, a patient and sometimes impatient waiting. Within Advent, this takes form in the way the season builds in intensity. We hear this in the scriptures of the Sundays, see it in the growing brightness of the Advent wreath, hear it in the last seven or nine days that are given to such things as the "O" antiphons (O Emmanuel, O Root of Jesse, O Desire of nations) and the posadas processions as Mary and Joseph look for hospitality. In the classroom, avoid the reds and greens. Go with the colors of winter, purples and blues, silver and white. Let the words and sounds of Christmas wait. Advent has its own lovely words and sounds.

CLASSROOM PREPARATION

In the school community, Advent needs expression in the daily prayer of the classroom: the special readings and songs and perhaps the Advent wreath. It needs also some public signs that this is a very different time (different from other parts of the year, different from what's going on in the stores). This might be a weekly eucharist or a school-wide prayer service around the school's large Advent wreath. Much about such liturgies would remain the same for all the weeks of Advent, but much also will show the way this season changes as the year moves toward its shortest days and longest nights, the time when Christians celebrate the feast of the nativity of the Lord.

The notes below on preparation have to do with the Advent season itself. There is this difference between the liturgy of Advent and the liturgies earlier in the year. For those feast days, there needs to be a preparation every year, building on the years before and leading up to the celebration of the liturgy. But Advent is itself a preparatory season. During November we can note when it is beginning, mark it on the calendar. But it comes when it comes and that will be the time for any discussions and activities that relate to Advent. The liturgy of one Advent is our preparation for the liturgy of the next. Once the season arrives, the use of "O come, O come, Emmanuel" or other music every day in the classroom will itself be rehearsal for the eucharistic liturgies.

Primary

Share stories about waiting—for a person, a visit, something special. How does it feel to wait? An Advent calendar (of good quality) can be part of the classroom preparation each day. Care and attention to the gifts that will be given to parents or to the elderly is Advent time well spent. Children can grasp quite well that the gift of time is precious and that they have this gift to give to others. There are many fine children's stories about waiting (e.g., *Charlotte's Web* has passages that make it a fine Advent story).

Intermediate

Here also the *preparation* of simple gifts and the understanding of the gift of time can be a focus. The season provides an opportunity to retell many stories from the Hebrew Scriptures and elsewhere, stories of promise and waiting. These are not a make-believe that Jesus has not come, to be forgotten as soon as we celebrate Christmas. Rather, they are about how we are waiting now. Find the dates for Chanukah, read the book of Maccabees and study how Chanukah is observed.

Junior High

These students could prepare a huge Advent calendar for the whole school. Each day's opening could show various pictures of the good works that lead to Christmas, with the whole of the calendar making a great mural of our way to the festival. Junior high students can also be responsible for the preparation of the school's main Advent wreath and for a presentation of the "O" antiphons on Advent's last days.

LITURGY PREPARATION

The darkness outside can be reflected in the subdued environment of the worship space. A beautiful, highly visible Advent wreath, perhaps placed in the midst of the assembly rather than beside the altar, can be a focal point. On the first school day of Advent, the whole community might gather for the blessings of this wreath (or of another wreath if this one will be seen only at the liturgies and there is to be a wreath in some central place in the school where it will be seen each day). An appropriate blessing ritual can be found in *Catholic Household Blessings and Prayers.*

The procession, whether of the whole community or of the ministers, can include a few bell ringers and those chosen to light the candle(s) of the wreath. The singing of "O come, O come, Emmanuel" (page 166) will immediately associate these days with past Advents and with the Advent Sunday liturgies. If all of the verses are not sung at each liturgy, the overall plan for the three or four liturgies of Advent should allow for different verses on different days. The homilist ought to pay attention to which verses are sung because the text may find good use in the homily.

Though "O come, O come, Emmanuel" will nearly always find some spot in the liturgies of Advent, there are other songs that would be excellent for the entrance: "Prepare the way of the Lord" (page 174) is a refrain that can be sung continuously. "Soon and very soon" (page 190) gives word and tune to another side of the Advent season.

When the procession arrives at the place of the wreath, the presider leads the sign of the cross and greets the assembly. Then in silence the proper number of candles are lighted on the wreath. After the lighting, a final verse of the song may be sung as the procession continues to the chair. Then the presider invites "Let us pray" and after the usual silence, reads the opening prayer.

The Advent season has a wealth of good readings from scripture. Once it is known how many liturgies the community will celebrate, turn to the lectionary and pore over the readings for the weekdays of Advent. Choose the readings for all the liturgies so that together they express something of the building anticipation of the season. The normal patterns of reading/silence/psalm/alleluia/gospel is kept, keeping both readings (perhaps especially the gospels) rather brief. The psalm could be Psalm 24 or Psalm 25 (both refrains are on page 58). The Alleluia could be one that is chosen for use only in Advent and during Christmastime. If the parish's Sunday liturgies have such an Alleluia (one not used the rest of the year), that will ordinarily be the best choice.

The homilist can help the children think about this season of the year: the dark, the cold, the dying down of the year. Many of these images will be reflected in the scriptures and in the songs of Advent. The characters we read about or listen to—especially Isaiah, John the Baptist and Mary—should be invited regularly into these Advent homilies. The focus of anticipation should be the whole Christmas season that culminates with Epiphany.

If the children are involved in gathering gifts for the poor, their liturgies can be the focus for this. The general directives for the Mass state that the collection is taken up for the church and for the poor. This is done while the table is being prepared. Perhaps it is best if any gifts are gathered first in the classrooms and brought to the worship space in large boxes, then brought forward at this time.

If the eucharist is celebrated twice or more during Advent, this may be the opportunity to reintroduce the second eucharistic prayer for Masses with children with its excellent pattern of proclamation and acclamation. Two settings for the children's acclamations are provided in the *Hymnal*. If one of the usual memorial acclamations is used, a setting of "When we eat this bread" is appropriate for Advent with its conclusion: ". . . until you come in glory." One setting for this is given on page 43. Also for special emphasis in Advent is the Lord's Prayer with the text that follows: ". . . as we wait in joyful hope . . ." Perhaps in Advent this can be sung.

Because much new music is being introduced (reintroduced from past Advents), the communion song might be the same as that used earlier in the fall. If something new is used, it might be one of the psalms mentioned above or "Prepare the way of the Lord."

The liturgy might conclude without a final song but, if possible, with instrumental music.

December 8: The Immaculate Conception

BACKGROUND

This is perhaps the only one of the great Marian feasts that will often fall on a school day (August 15 coming in summer and January 1 on a school holiday). This feast comes not as a disruption or intermission in Advent, but very much as a manifestation of what Advent means in the church. This will carry through in both the classroom preparation and the liturgy of the feast. This is a Holy Day. Other parishioners will probably be celebrating the liturgy with the children. Plan for mutual hospitality.

CLASSROOM PREPARATION

The image of Mary is central all through Advent and Christmas-time. Preparing for the Immaculate Conception, then, is not a separate task. It means that at all levels the scripture texts and songs and prayers appropriate to this feast should be integrated into the classroom in the early days of Advent. Special efforts in the early grades might be made with learning the prayers to Mary on pages 215–16 of the *Hymnal*. Any of these texts should be learned in a context of scripture stories.

Older children could spend time with Mary's Magnificat. This poem is a part of the church's evening prayer every day and is found in "Prayer at the End of the Day" (page 16 in the *Hymnal*). Look up the scriptural context in Luke 1. It comes in the story of Mary's visit to Elizabeth. Here would be an Advent activity in imitation of Mary: surprise visits to the homebound. The Magnificat would be an important text for older students to commit to memory either in the metrical setting (as in the *Hymnal*) or in a translation that is more faithful to the original. The Magnificat on page 158 of the *Hymnal* uses the first Latin words of this prayer as a refrain. Because the word "Magnificat" remains in English as the title of the prayer, it would be good for students to learn this lovely melody.

In connection with these prayers and scriptures, the Marian hymns should be sung and discussed in preparation for the feast. "Sing of Mary" and "Immaculate Mary" are possible choices for this, but give first place to the Magnificat.

LITURGY PREPARATION

The liturgy should follow the same format as the other liturgies of Advent (lighting of the Advent wreath, same psalm and acclamations) using the scriptures assigned to this day and a Marian hymn at the beginning and/or the conclusion.

Christmastime Liturgy

BACKGROUND

If little by little the children gain some notion of Advent as a time of waiting, a time of promise and expectation, then they will be able to celebrate a Christmas that is not over on December 26 but lasts through Epiphany and until the feast of the Baptism of the Lord. If they have kept Advent, then when they return from the Christmas vacation, it is time for the Christmas parties. During the days until the Baptism of the Lord (usually the second Sunday in January, but not always: check the calendar) the daily prayer in the classroom should include prayers and songs of Christmastime.

Within these days, Christmastime should be celebrated at a eucharist. This is not an effort to repeat the Christmas Day Mass in the school setting. Rather, it is simply a manifestation of how

Christmas Day begins a season called Christmastime, and within that season we celebrate for many days that the Word was made flesh and lived among us. Sometimes January 6, the traditional day for Epiphany, will be a good choice for the liturgy. Then the songs and scriptures of Epiphany can be used. The season has a richness of scripture and of song that will be manifest on whatever day is chosen.

CLASSROOM PREPARATION

As noted for Advent, these seasonal liturgies do not take the same sort of classroom preparation as the feast days kept in the fall. Instead, it is the very presence of the season in many aspects of school and classroom life that prepares for the liturgy. The liturgy's songs may be used ahead of time in the classroom prayer—right from the first day after Christmas vacation.

The timing of the Christmastime eucharist will determine much about preparation and follow-up. On the days before January 6, when we are still within the 12 days of Christmas, particular stories may be read and told in the classroom as part of preparation for the liturgy. These can be the legends of particular peoples that surround Christmastime. (Some of these are beautifully told in Ruth Sawyer's *This Way to Christmas,* a book that is difficult to find but well worth the effort. The Christmas story is retold in the manner of black Africa in *Every Man Heart Lay Down.* Some of the legends of Christmas have been beautifully illustrated in books for primary and intermediate children.)

If the date for the liturgy is January 6 or after, then the stories and songs of Epiphany should be worked with in the classroom. The story of the Magi has been elaborately dramatized in such works as *Amahl and the Night Visitors* and embellished in stories like "The Other Wise Man." The story can also be done and embellished all over again by any group of children. Teachers should know also that our feast of Epiphany has long been a celebration of more than the Magi. It has been the occasion to retell the stories of the wedding feast and Cana and of Jesus' baptism in the Jordan by John. All of these manifestations come together and all of the stories should be very familiar.

LITURGY PREPARATION

The brightness of many candles should mark the transition from Advent. The Advent wreath has become a Christmas wreath with many lights (of the Christmas tree variety if not actual candles) shining to mark the celebration of Emmanuel, God with us. If the liturgy is celebrated in the parish church, all of the trees and flowers, as well as the crèche, should be in their places and brightly lighted. Especially if the celebration will center on the Epiphany, then the most fragrant incense ought to be present, burning beside the crèche and carried in the censer for use in the liturgy.

The procession, of some or all, is festive with the light and incense and the singing. "O come, all ye faithful" (page 164, with some of the older children learning the first verse in Latin) or "Songs of thankfulness and praise" (page 188) are appropriate. The latter should not be used unless it has become well known to all through practice or from the Sunday liturgy. The Gloria, in the Taizé version (page 128), would be a different kind of procession music; some of the children might be prepared to use bells and other percussion with it. Or the entire Gloria might be sung within the entrance rite; this can be done with a cantor singing most of the text and the children doing a refrain (see the Gloria on page 74 of the *Hymnal*). The procession can pause at the crèche; the presider leads the sign of the cross and the greeting and welcome. Then the procession and singing continue. The entrance concludes, when all are at their places, with the opening prayer.

The scripture may be one of those from Christmas Day that are heard less often (the Mass at Dawn or the Mass during the Day) or it could be all or part of Matthew's telling of the story of the Magi and the Holy Innocents. Near the end of the Christmastime, the stories of the baptism of Jesus and of the wedding at Cana could also be appropriate. The homilist would then have the special task of showing how the Christmas songs and decor all lead to these stories of water-made-wine and the doings at the Jordan River. The responsorial psalm for Christmastime is Psalm 98; the *Hymnal* gives two antiphons on pages 62 and 63.

Homilists should beware of the "what did you get" approach to a Christmas homily. "What did you give" may be better. Go over to the crèche again and talk about what all this manger and shepherds business was all about.

This would be an occasion to bring up plenty of incense with the gifts and then to honor the assembly with its fragrant smoke.

The eucharistic prayer would best be done as during Advent. For communion, there are a number of Christmas carols that have refrains; these are well suited to use in the procession: "Angels we have heard on high," "What child is this," "The first Noel," and "O come, all ye faithful" are the best-known possibilities.

Good songs to conclude the liturgy are "Go tell it on the mountain" and "Joy to the world." These, as well as most of those mentioned above, will be found in the *Hymnal*. The procession from the room could be for everyone and could lead to a bright Christmas tree laden with candy canes—the Christmastime continues.

January: Praying for Peace and Christian Unity

The month of January brings a number of concerns before us. In a way, they are all closely bound to our celebration of Christmas. As a nation, we celebrate the birthday of Dr. Martin Luther King, Jr., on the third Monday of January. At about that same time, we mark a week of prayer for Christian unity. The church also calls on us to pray for peace in the world as we begin each new year. And finally, Catholic Schools Week is celebrated in January in many places.

In the classroom or in larger assemblies, these occasions can be marked with prayer services. This should happen only if there is something more going on in the parish or the school. This could involve study: the life and work of Dr. King, now available in many books for different age levels, the continuation of struggle for racial justice; the story of the separation of the churches, what is special to other Christian denominations in the local community, the work of ecumenism; the work of peacemakers in the world today, especially the work of the United Nations and the teachings of the church and of the United States bishops on peace (as found especially in their pastoral letter, *The Challenge of Peace*); the history of this school, the reasons it exists and the means by which it exists. The study, in some cases, could lead to activities and projects such as letter writing on behalf of legislation to correct injustice. When such things happen, then there is cause for a prayer service.

Resources for such prayer services can be gathered from the parish and the diocese. Talk to the diocesan Peace and Justice Office about materials for the observance of Dr. King's birthday and prayers for world peace; talk to the diocesan school office about Catholic Schools Week; talk to the office for ecumenism about materials on and prayers for Christian unity.

The structure of the prayer service can be drawn from the general form used in this book: song with sign of the cross and greeting and opening prayer; scripture reading with a psalm and homily; intercessions; the Lord's Prayer; blessing; song. Sometimes an appropriate gesture (e.g., an offering of letters about an important issue of justice or peace) can be part of the service.

Many appropriate psalms and songs for these days can be found in the *Hymnal*. Among them are "In Christ there is no East or West" (page 141) and "We shall overcome" (page 203). Other suggestions are found in the "Index of Music" in this volume.

Appropriate scriptures are many. These would include: Isaiah 2:1–5 for Dr. King's birthday; John 17:20–23 for Christian unity; Luke 18:15–17 for Catholic Schools Week; Luke 1:46–55 for world peace.

The prayers of intercession should offer the children an opportunity to list the many concerns related to each of these occasions.

February 2: The Presentation of the Lord

BACKGROUND

Forty days after Christmas, the church tells the story of the presentation of Jesus in the Temple. It is an ancient feast that comes on a day that some peoples have taken to be one of the turning points of the year. Even our Groundhog Day tradition testifies that people have found February 2 a time to take a deep breath and think about the end of winter. So, while darkness still holds more hours than daylight but there is every hope of spring, the church has kept this feast with the place of worship full of lights: It is Candlemas (candle-Mass) Day!

The story of the presentation in the Temple is part of the infancy story told in Luke's gospel. In some ways, then, this feast is the conclusion of Advent/Christmastime, or at least a sort of echo of that festivity. The central text of this day has often been the words of Simeon: "My eyes have seen your salvation, which you prepared in sight of all the peoples, a light for revelation to the Gentiles, and glory for your people Israel." The notions of darkness and light, which resounded all through Advent and Christmas, return now and are brought to a wonderful conclusion in the words of Simeon and the blessing of candles.

If the children are part of the assembly for the parish's principal liturgy on this day, then that liturgy is to begin with a blessing of candles and a procession. The sacramentary provides an introduction to this (under the liturgy for February 2) and texts for the prayers. Even if the procession cannot be done, the liturgy is still to begin with a blessing of candles.

CLASSROOM PREPARATION

The gospel story and the songs chosen for February 2 should work their way into the days that lead up to this liturgy. In some cases, even with younger students, this will be an occasion to talk about what we mean when we "bless" something. We say that in making the sign of the cross we bless ourselves. At the end of the Mass, the presider blesses everyone present. We encourage parents to bless their children. Before a meal, we bless ourselves and we bless the food—or rather, we ask God to bless us and the gifts we are about to receive. And we have the times when the church asks us to join and bless something or to ask God's blessing on something: the fields at springtime, these candles on February 2, the couple on their wedding day, the body of one who has died and the grave in which that body will be laid.

There are many notions tied up in blessing, notions that go back into the scriptures where we have God blessing Abraham and Abraham blessing God. Rather than trying to pin down exactly what it means to bless something or somebody, it would be good to open up how vast and important this notion is. It is as simple as what happens when someone sneezes and someone else responds: "God bless you," but it may take a form as elaborate as this blessing of candles or even the blessing of a home or a church.

Primary

Talk with the children about light, about the different kinds of light, and about all that light does for us. Find the scripture text where Jesus says, "I am the light of the world." And where Jesus says: "You are the light of the world." Is Jesus light for us? Are we light for one another? Learn to sing "This little light of mine," and perhaps to put gestures with it. Darken the room for a little while on these days and light a single beautiful candle. Sit quietly by its light.

Intermediate

Explore the way candles and light are used in the liturgy of the church. Why continue to do something that is not practical anymore? Talk about candles in the procession, at the gospel, around the altar, before the tabernacle and before icons and statues. Talk about the new fire of the Easter Vigil and the paschal candle at funerals and baptisms. Go and look at these candles. Talk about the different materials that may be used in making candles. Perhaps the students could help select and decorate the candles that will be given to newly baptized infants and adults during the coming year.

Junior high

The junior high students could collect the stubs of all the Christmas candles and could bring additional stubs from home and from friends. Under the guidance of one who has experience in making candles, they could work in small groups to melt these candles and to make new candles for Candlemas Day. Students of this age could also be challenged to learn by heart the few verses of the Canticle of Simeon (Luke 2:29–32) and to use it each night as a bedside prayer.

LITURGY PREPARATION

The solemn procession and blessing of candles given in the sacramentary for February 2 can be the format for this day's unusual entrance rite. If the students have not made their own candles, they can be invited to bring candles from home to be blessed, and all of the candles to be used in the church in the coming year—vigil lights, candles for Mass, baptismal candles—can be brought together for this blessing.

The liturgy begins in a room away from the church or in some part of the church away from the altar. All gather around the candles and, if possible, all hold unlighted candles. Then in silence begin to light some of the candles and to sing. "This little light of mine" (page 196) is one possibility; others are "I want to walk as a child of the light" (page 138) or "We are walking in the light" (page 199). Or a psalm refrain may be sung and then repeated again at communion; Psalm 27 ("The Lord is my light," page 59) or Psalm 98 (an echo of Christmas with the refrain, "All the ends of the earth have seen . . .") would be possibilities.

When the candles are lighted, the presider greets everyone and announces the feast. The words suggested in the sacramentary serve as an example of what can be said. Then the presider blesses all the candles and sprinkles them with holy water. It may seem a fitting gesture to take incense and honor the candles with its fragrant clouds of smoke.

Then all go in procession, carrying candles and picking up the song that began the liturgy. If lighted candles pose too many problems, the children could carry the unlighted candles that will be used by the church during the year ahead.

When all arrive at the place for the liturgy, the candles are collected by persons assigned to this. The presider invites all to pray and, after silence, speaks the opening prayer.

It may be best on this occasion to have a single reading, the gospel story of the presentation, with an alleluia sung before and after. A very brief homily can ponder with the children the gospel story and some of the words they have been singing, as well as the beauty of the candles and their light. Talk about how this place sees, has seen and will see so many burning candles, from the tiny vigil lights that are like our prayers to the great paschal candle of Eastertime and baptisms and funerals.

The eucharistic prayer could well repeat the format of Advent and Christmastime. Song for the communion procession was mentioned above. All could process out singing "This little light of mine."

Ash Wednesday

BACKGROUND
In the days before Lent, everyone (teachers, administration, students) should sense the invitation to consider the ways to keep Lent. Not all of this is for the individual. The classroom community can decide some things about their lenten prayer, about how they will practice fasting (something that is and should be presented as very positive), about how they will practice charity (almsgiving, like fasting, can take hundreds of forms). Lent need never be presented as a burden. It is a challenge, a struggle, an opportunity, an invitation, an exciting time for the church every year.

All of this will come about when teachers and students have a sense for why they would be setting aside 40 days in the first place. That sense comes from experience. Each year we have a little more notion because we have done it one more time. At the heart of Lent is what comes when Lent ends: the Three Days (Triduum) that begin on the night of Holy Thursday and end on Easter Sunday evening. This is the church's celebration of the passover of the Lord Jesus. It is the time when we are asked to leave aside life as usual and enter into prayer and vigiling until, on the night between Saturday and Sunday, the death and resurrection of the Lord are proclaimed in word and song and, especially, in the baptism of new Christians. That baptism, in which there is death and life forever in the Lord, is the whole meaning of Lent and of Eastertime.

All preparation for Lent is to be mindful of these catechumens coming toward the end of their journey, coming to baptism. The great importance of that journey and the power and beauty of baptism should be the great image of all the days from Ash Wednesday to Pentecost. Without this, Lent can become just a time to be endured, a time to use just any ideas and themes. For those who are baptized, baptism is a center to Lent. It comes to us through all Lent's scriptures and stories, its music and its observances. (For a more thorough discussion of this season, see the pamphlet "An Introduction to Lent and Eastertime," published by Liturgy Training Publications.) As the children learn that Lent is going somewhere—to the Vigil with its fire, candle, scriptures, font, oil and eucharist—they should learn to look forward to attending the liturgies of the Triduum with their families. Just before the Triduum, the children can be involved in a spring cleaning of school and church, putting all in readiness for the Triduum and Eastertime.

More than any other season or feast, the days that begin on Ash Wednesday, climax in the Triduum and continue until Pentecost need to be carefully considered each year by teachers. Good school customs can be kept year after year. The more frequent celebration of the weekday eucharistic liturgy may be such a practice. The eucharistic liturgy every Wednesday or Friday, for example, may well be part of the keeping of Lent. (However, if this is done during Lent, then weekly eucharist should also be part of the keeping of Eastertime. That is the often-neglected season when the wonder of our baptism overflows into a whole 50 days.) Such a weekly celebration of the eucharist would mean a careful effort to use the lenten and Eastertime liturgies that are given below (following the Ash Wednesday notes). Each of Lent's Masses should follow the same format, varying only in the readings and homily and perhaps in some verses of hymns. The same will be true of Eastertime.

CLASSROOM PREPARATION

The lenten disciplines of prayer, fasting and almsgiving—in all their many forms—can be carried on by the whole school community. Avoid competition ("Who brought in the most canned goods this week?") and emphasize how a community working together can do so much more than any one of us alone.

Younger students can prepare by bringing in the palm branches from last year. Treat these branches with reverence, remembering and discussing how they were blessed and used on Palm Sunday. Keep them in a special place of honor until Ash Wednesday.

Older students could look into and report on the celebration of Mardi Gras in various parts of the world. What have communities done before going into Lent? What importance does the climate and the food supply have? Why the masks? Then they can plan a carnival (and it should be on Mardi Gras—Fat Tuesday—not some anticipated day) for the school: masks, music, treats, games, a parade with an entry from each classroom.

LITURGY PREPARATION

The service that follows is for Ash Wednesday. It presumes that the liturgy of that day will be celebrated apart from the Mass. It can easily be adapted when ashes are to be blessed and distributed within Mass.

Ashes are a powerful symbol. Let them speak for themselves on this day. Palm branches from the previous year can be brought by the children in the days before Ash Wednesday with the knowledge that these will become this year's ashes. The homilist should be reflecting on why we would turn these branches to ashes, and why we would rub those ashes into our bodies.

A brazier or thick kettle can be used for the burning of pieces of palm just before the liturgy itself. A small container should be on hand for the ashes when they have cooled. Before the liturgy, cut into small pieces some of the palms brought by the children. A few children could be designated to bring these pieces of palm forward. The smell of burning palms will be a memorable part of this liturgy.

The space for this and all lenten liturgies should be uncluttered. Use only the essentials. Lighting should be subdued, setting a tone of anticipation and preparation.

Those who take part in this service should be second graders and older children. Younger children could have an even simpler service of their own.

Because this is not given here as a eucharist, the presider may be a layperson.

Begin in silence with the sign of the cross made slowly and without any words. Then pieces of palm are brought forward and the presider sets them ablaze. (This first part of the service could be done outside, coming inside afterwards with the ashes. Or it can be done inside providing the space allows for this fire.) During the burning, a song can be sung (e.g., "O breathe on me, O breath of God"—any songs chosen for today should be carried through into Lent, both in the classroom and at liturgies). After the palms have been burned, the presider may speak briefly of what has happened: last year's palm becoming this year's ashes. Then the presider invites "Let us pray," and, after the silence, reads the opening prayer.

If a procession takes place from the place of the fire to the place of the service, a flute or an oboe might lead everyone, playing one of the melodies that will be sung later.

At the place of the service, all are seated for the word. Read a single scripture from the lectionary for Ash Wednesday. In the homily, speak very briefly of how we all together—adults and children, bishops and people, baptized and catechumens—today enter into Lent. We do this marked with ashes. Talk about ashes and how they are a very strong sign of our belief that God can bring life where there is none. We have our Lent ahead of us, the struggle inside and outside against evil. Our weapons are prayer and all variety of fasting and almsgiving—and God's grace.

After the homily the ashes are simply but solemnly blest and the children come forward to receive them. This should be without any haste so that the marking with the ashes and the words can both be clear and strong for each child. Other adult ministers (who should be present for the whole liturgy) may assist with the ashes, but they should be rehearsed in this. And all adults, presider included, should also receive ashes. A song such as "Jesu, Jesu" (page 143) may be used with all joining in the refrain. The song could be repeated at each lenten liturgy and certainly used on Holy Thursday morning.

The prayers of intercession today, and throughout Lent, might be especially inclusive: many brief intentions that include the many needs and persons we bring with us to Lent. Singing the intercessions is appropriate anytime, but might be introduced in the lenten liturgies.

The liturgy concludes with the Lord's Prayer and final blessing. A silent conclusion is possible, or all might sing a song that will be heard throughout Lent (e.g., "Lord, who throughout these forty days," page 156).

Lenten Liturgy

BACKGROUND

See the notes above for Ash Wednesday. The liturgy outlined here is intended to serve for a eucharist celebrated weekly, or at least several times, during Lent. Because the Fridays of Lent have long had special significance attached to them, this may be the best choice of a day for weekly eucharist. There may be good reasons for choosing not to have the eucharist this often, but some assembly for prayer should mark each week of Lent and of Eastertime also.

CLASSROOM PREPARATION

As in any season, the basic preparation for the liturgy is the many ways in which simply being in Lent marks daily life. This would especially be seen in the daily prayer where the song and the scripture readings would give a presence to Lent. The joy and the brightness of Lent, a joy that flows from Lent's disciplines and the freedom they bring, need to be manifest in teachers. The solidarity of the church in its Lent becomes real in the ways in which teachers, students, parish staff and all the people of the parish are in this journey together.

If the practice does not exist year-round, this might be the opportunity to introduce classroom time each week to listen to the scriptures that will be read at Mass on the next Sunday, or to look back on last Sunday's readings. In Lent, the gospels of nearly every Sunday are among the finest stories the church has to tell, but they take preparation and follow-through. Some of these lend themselves to mime and drama.

Because all of Lent leads to the Easter Vigil and its baptismal font, these days involve all sorts of ways to be baptized people: to act like baptized people act, to think like baptized people think, to sing like baptized people sing. In Eastertime we will sing, "You have put on Christ." All the deeds of Lent, all its alms and silence and scripture, are our slow putting on of Christ. Children are, in a way, only minor characters in Lent. It's an adult activity. There is a danger in trivializing Lent if it appears to be children's activities organized by adults. The only way to have a Lent in a school community is for it to be the full and serious pursuit of the adult community (teachers, administration, parents) in which the children can share to some extent. Lent makes it very clear that a school is only part of a larger community, the parish (and the diocese), from which it derives its identity.

Look for simple ways that Lent's disciplines and its liturgy can be expressed. Certainly Lent is a time when we intensify our prayer of intercession. This prayer—which in the ancient church was done only by the baptized after the catechumens had been sent forth—is something we do each Sunday at Mass in the prayer of the faithful and in a little way each day as we ask God to bless parents and grandparents, brothers and sisters, friends and enemies. Intercession is a job—both a privilege and a responsibility—of every baptized person. How do we learn to do this? One way is Lent. Not only could the intercessions for daily prayer in the classroom and for Mass be prepared with special care (which is not the same thing as making them long), but children can practice the discipline of intercession. One part of that is just learning to keep our eyes open and learning where in the world to look. What should a Christian be watching? How can we get our attention and our prayer on the places where there are troubles? Pictures and words gathered by the children into a strong presence in the classroom can become the source of intercession. Such words and pictures from the immediate community (always including the catechumens) to the world community become a backdrop for listening to and discussion of Lent's scriptures.

LITURGY PREPARATION

The place for the lenten liturgy should be uncluttered in every way. Absence can speak strongly. The church gets down to basics: the reading stand with its book, the table with its bread and wine.

Any procession might be omitted with a real effort to gather in silence, the ministers taking their places even before the children arrive. A sung Kyrie might begin while they are still taking their places (learning the meaning of the ancient "Kyrie eleison" would be part of Lent and a yearly bond to Christians of many centuries). The ministers might be kneeling and the children would take the same posture. The entrance rites for other seasons and feasts have not included the penitential rite, but here it would constitute the greater part of this rite. When all are in their places, the presider rises and leads the sign of the cross, then greets the assembly. Some simple words of invitation lead to a continuation of the Kyrie as the presider kneels again. This time, specific acclamations (e.g., "Lord Jesus, you have shown us God's strong love; Lord, have mercy") would be included as usual in the penitential rite. A short silence might separate one petition from the next. At the end of this penitential rite, all rise and the presider says, "May almighty God have mercy . . ." Then the opening prayer is done as usual.

If during these days the morning or afternoon prayer in the classroom is somewhat extended with more reading of the scriptures and if the eucharist is being celebrated each week, then it may be wise to use only one scripture (the gospel) and to keep a certain brevity to these lenten Masses. The weekday lectionary for Lent should be consulted in choosing a gospel reading, but the Sunday gospels may be worth repeating, though perhaps using only a portion of them. Many of these are the great catechetical stories and they offer the homilist an opportunity to unfold basic elements of the faith.

Thus the liturgy of the word might consist in the singing of a psalm, the gospel (without the usual procession and without incense, but with its special lenten acclamation, "Praise to you, Lord Jesus Christ," instead of the alleluia), the homily and the intercessions (as suggested, these might be in a special sung form). The psalm can be Psalm 51 (page 60) or Psalm 91 (page 61). Whichever is used, it should become familiar through daily use of the refrain in classroom prayer.

If the acclamations of the second eucharistic prayer for Masses with children were learned in Advent, they can be used now throughout Lent. If they have not been learned yet, now would be the time to introduce them when they can become familiar through use week after week. The presider and the instrumentalist or cantor are crucial in giving this eucharistic prayer its character. This character is in the back-and-forth, the dialogue of proclamation (by the presider) and acclamation (by all). This should be sensed in every eucharistic prayer, but the special patterns of the second eucharistic prayer for Masses with children bring it out best.

The song for the communion procession could be either of the psalms mentioned above. Other possibilities include: "We remember" (page 200), "Jesus, remember me" (page 145), "Somebody's knockin' " (page 186) or "Were you there" (page 204). All of these use either a refrain or have the sort of repetition that makes a book unnecessary.

The closing might be in silence, but there are also good hymns to be sung: "Amazing grace" (page 108), "Again we keep this solemn fast" (page 99), "Lord, who throughout these forty days" (page 156). "Lift high the cross" (page 154), used on the feast of the Holy Cross in September, could also be a theme song used many times in Lent and even repeated in Eastertime.

Lenten Penance/Reconciliation Service

BACKGROUND

The *Hymnal* includes the order for the rite of penance celebrated as a communal reconciliation service. Use of this will depend on the practice of the parish and the diocese. Such a service may be held for individual classes, for groups of classes or for all the older students together. The service may be, as outlined, with time for individual confession and absolution, or it may be without individual confession and absolution. In some cases, it will seem better to invite the older students to attend the parish services of reconciliation with their parents.

CLASSROOM PREPARATION

Those who prepare the liturgy of penance and those who prepare children to attend this liturgy should work together. It is best if the order of the service found in the Rite of Penance is closely followed; the elements of this resemble the introductory rites and the liturgy of the word familiar from the eucharist. Lent itself is the basic preparation for participation in the penance service. The season itself makes us conscious of the struggle against evil and of our own failures. Study the Confiteor (which older students should now know by heart) and the Prayer of Contrition (page 218), as well as the scriptures and songs that are used at the penance service. These are our best teachers. This study becomes an occasion to talk about how night prayer has been for Christians a daily moment to look back over the day and express sorrow before God for those times "I have sinned through my own fault, in my thoughts and in my words, in what I have done, and in what I have failed to do." The Confiteor or another brief prayer may be taught as part of the night prayer for both children and adults.

If the rite is to be celebrated with confession and absolution, study the words of absolution (given on page 53 of the *Hymnal*) and discuss the meaning of the gesture that is used, the laying on of hands. Find the places in the scriptures where this is a gesture of healing. In the case of such a service, emphasize that it is always the choice of the individual Christian to approach the priest for confession. At all levels, the preparation for the penance service should be of a piece with the observance of Lent. Specific catechesis about the sacrament should draw on the best approaches taken in the religious education materials in use in the school.

LITURGY PREPARATION

If the service is to include private confession and absolution, the order of service is:

> Introductory Rites
>> Song
>> Greeting
>> (words of invitation and instruction)
>
> Liturgy of the Word
>> First reading
>> Psalm
>> Second reading
>> Acclamation
>> Gospel

> Homily
> Examination of conscience
> Rite of Reconciliation
> General confession
> Song or litany
> Lord's Prayer
> Individual confession and absolution
> Proclamation of praise for God's mercy
> Prayer of thanksgiving
> Concluding Rite
> Blessing
> Dismissal

This order is taken from the Rite of Penance, Form II. It could be used as well when individual confession and absolution are not to be part of the service, simply omitting that one element. In any case, the liturgy of the word could be simplified as is usual at children's liturgies. The Rite of Penance (Appendix II, Part I) provides full descriptions and texts for two models of a lenten penance service without individual confession and absolution. These can be very helpful, but the suggestions made there must be integrated into the whole order of service given above when individual confession and absolution are to be included. This Appendix II to the Rite of Penance also offers a model service "for young people" (number 55 through number 61); this also may provide some texts or insights that will be of use in preparing the lenten service.

The scripture readings should be carefully chosen and perhaps prepared by small groups of children for mime or drama if this can be done well. The psalm and gospel acclamation can be those familiar from the lenten eucharistic liturgies. The homilist brings together the season, the scriptures and the specific classroom preparation that has gone into this service. The words of the psalm that is being used throughout Lent may be another important text for the homilist: just a single verse pondered in the homily and offered to the children as a daily lenten prayer or a night prayer for year-round.

The homily is followed by a time of examination of conscience. Appendix III to the Rite of Penance provides some models for this that should be adapted to the age of the children. This will usually take a litany form: short statements or questions followed by a brief time of silence.

The communal dimension of this liturgy is strongly present in what follows. The General Confession need not be long but it should be central to this service. All kneel for a prayer of confession. This may be the Confiteor recited with great attention. Then all stand for a litany or song. Two examples of such litanies are found in number 34 of the Rite of Penance; the refrain might be the Kyrie familiar from lenten Masses. In many cases, a song would be preferred here to a litany: for example, "I want to walk as a child of the light" (page 138), "Jesu, Jesu" (page 143), "Now we remain" (page 160), "What wondrous love is this" (page 208). A lenten song that would be very appropriate is "O sun of justice" (page 172).

Individual confession follows. The Rite of Penance gives this rubric for the confession:

> Then the penitents go to the priests designated for individual confession, and confess their sins. Each one receives and accepts a fitting act of satisfaction and is absolved. After hearing the confession and offering suitable counsel, the priest extends his hands over the penitent's head (or at least extends his right hand) and gives absolution. Everything else which is customary in individual confession is omitted.

As much as possible, this time is to be integral to the service. It is not an interruption. Nor should the rest of the rite appear as only some minor preliminary to the individual confessions. The service is a whole. This can be the sense of things if there is an adequate number of confessors. Anything that suggests "lining up" of every student for confession should be avoided. It may be best if at this time the students are asked to move apart and find a quiet place to sit.

When the confessions have been completed, all come back together. The presider speaks briefly, inviting all to give thanks and to do good works. Everyone can then join in a psalm or song in praise of God's mercy. Something lively and rousing is in place: for example, "Shout for joy, loud and long" (page 178), "Sing a new song" (page 179), "The Lord, the Lord, the Lord is my shepherd" (page 194). The presider speaks the concluding prayer (number 57 of the Rite of Penance offers a long and a short option; the short one is better). Then the blessing and dismissal conclude the service. No concluding song is needed.

Holy Thursday

BACKGROUND
Lent ends on the evening of Holy Thursday as the church enters the Paschal Triduum, the three days from Thursday evening to Sunday evening that are the center of the year for us. The liturgies of the

Triduum are to be celebrated only once in every parish unless there are very exceptional circumstances (such as more people coming than will fit in the church). The liturgy of Holy Thursday evening, therefore, is not to be anticipated earlier in the day with a school Mass. Having kept Lent, the children should be invited now to attend the liturgies of the Triduum and to keep the Triduum in appropriate ways. This cannot happen unless the parish as a whole has a good sense of Lent and is now ready to keep Good Friday and Holy Saturday as days of vigiling and fasting and prayer, coming then to the great Easter Vigil liturgy in which the mystery of Jesus dead, buried and risen is celebrated. The Triduum climaxes around the waters as the catechumens are baptized, then anointed in confirmation and led to the eucharistic table. Easter Sunday then becomes a day of great joy and the first of the 50 days of Eastertime. The church makes clear that all of this is to be done by the parish as a whole. None of the liturgies (the Mass of Thursday night, the celebration of the Lord's passion on Friday or the Vigil on Saturday night) is to be celebrated more than once in any parish. The point is clear: Everyone is to come together at one time in one place for these liturgies.

In most cases, there will be no school on Good Friday. The task then is for children to understand (along with parents and the rest of the parish) the nature of these days. This is not just a day off. Nor is Good Friday the only day that matters: Both Friday and Saturday are treated by the church as days of fasting and prayer and keeping watch. All of this is to be conveyed to children by word and by example. Parents need help and encouragement from the parish and the school; they should be invited to come with their children to the parish liturgies of the Triduum.

LITURGY PREPARATION

In many cases, it will help if there is a way to bid Lent farewell during the day on Holy Thursday. In no way should such a final lenten service be an anticipation of the liturgy of Holy Thursday night. Whether held in the classroom or as a large assembly, this can be a modified form of the "Prayer at the End of the Day" or a very simple liturgy of the word. In either case, the music used would be the music of Lent. The liturgy of the word could be in this format:

> Gathering song (e.g., "Jesu, Jesu" on page 143, if this has been used during Lent; otherwise another familiar lenten song)
> Sign of the cross, greeting and prayer
> A reading from scripture (perhaps one of the sayings of Jesus about his passion, e.g., Matthew 20:17–19, Luke 18:31–33)

A homily looking back at the way all have tried to keep Lent
and inviting everyone now to enter with great attention and
excitement and anticipation into the Triduum (taking time
to explain words like "paschal" and "triduum")

Prayers of intercession, especially for the catechumens

The Lord's Prayer

The blessing (taken from the sacramentary, number 5 of the
solemn blessings, "The Passion of the Lord")

Quiet singing of "Jesus, remember me" (page 145) or another
refrain learned during Lent (this could be continued as
children depart one class at a time)

The homilist may use the invitation to the Triduum to speak
descriptively of what the church will be doing tonight and
tomorrow and at the Vigil: We will wash one another's feet as Jesus
did and will enter into a time of keeping watch; we will tomorrow
hear the reading of the passion and venerate the holy cross; we will
then continue our waiting and fasting and prayer through Saturday
until we gather that night to light a great fire and a magnificent
candle, to listen to the finest stories of our scripture, to bless the
waters of the font and to baptize the catechumens, then to anoint
them with chrism and bring them for the first time to the table of
the eucharist. These deeds are presented as the things that are done
by the adults of the parish. We are saying: You should know what
will be happening and even be present for some of it so that
someday you can continue this work.

With or without such a final lenten ritual, the last moments of
every Lent in the school might be devoted to getting the school,
church and grounds as clean as possible for the great days ahead.

Eastertime Liturgy

BACKGROUND

Eastertime is the 50 days from Easter Sunday to Pentecost Sunday. It
springs from the Triduum as the time to put time aside, the time to
live as if the reign of God had already arrived. In the early church,
fasting and kneeling were forbidden in these days because they
would make no sense in God's reign. But this is a hard season for us
to keep, at least until we get better at the Triduum itself and at Lent.
Then we will know what it is that prompts such rejoicing. For now,
though, we can be conscious of the spirit of this season and seek it
in scriptures and songs, in the very presence of the springtime
sights and smells, in lives of joy and charity.

Eastertime is also the time when the school year ends (usually before Pentecost, but this depends on the date of Easter). That means that it is easy to crowd out Eastertime. Yet things like graduations can be made a part of Eastertime. So can first communions and confirmation (this is the time above all others when these sacraments of initiation should be celebrated). So can May festivities in honor of Mary (after all, these are rites of spring and of fertility and Easter has room for all of this). Spring itself— longer and warmer days, colors, the feel of new life in cities as well as countryside—is a constant point of reference for celebrating Eastertime.

We need a sense for the continuity and wholeness of the time from Ash Wednesday to Pentecost. That will not be found when Lent is marked with much visual interest, much activity around almsgiving, weekly eucharist—and Eastertime is hardly marked at all. Eastertime needs attention and care. Like all the seasons, one year should repeat and build upon the last. When there has been a weekly Mass during Lent, this can be continued through Eastertime. The description below is suited to this. But attention should be given also to the ways Easter is seen and smelled in flowers and flowering branches in the classrooms and throughout the school. Easter is to be heard in prayer at the beginning and end of the day, especially in the way we sing extra alleluias in every nook and cranny of our prayer. Easter scriptures are to be read and studied and discussed. These scriptures would include those of the Sundays in Eastertime, but also—because many of the youngest children will not have been there—those of the Easter Vigil itself. And Easter will be found in the presence of blessed water as a daily reminder of our baptism: taking this water for the sign of the cross as part of prayer at the beginning or ending of the day, and keeping the water in a place of honor in the classroom throughout the season.

CLASSROOM PREPARATION

Once again, because this is a season, the preparation for the liturgy is something pervasive. The environment and the songs and the scriptures of the worship space are anticipated and echoed in the classroom. This takes care so that there is a freshness to the whole 50 days. Nothing is less like Easter than nearly dead Easter lilies.

The church is beginning to understand Eastertime (as was true in the early church) as a time when the newly baptized gathered to talk about all that they had experienced, especially the celebration of baptism, confirmation and eucharist. In a sense, all the children are newly baptized. Like all of us, they renew that baptism in the Easter liturgy. Now, for these 50 days, the classroom is a good place to unfold what we experience in baptism, confirmation and eucharist. This might mean for some a yearly contact with godparents by letter (even if they live close by). It might mean visits to the baptistry of the church and to the ambry (where the oils are kept). It might mean a yearly study of the Mass, especially the eucharistic prayer and the communion. It might mean having someone who was initiated at the Vigil come to talk with the children about what happened that night.

Primary
Children could be invited to bring photos of their own baptism and their baptism certificates and perhaps garments and candles. Discuss the promises parents made at baptism.

Intermediate
Students could make or decorate containers for holy water that would be filled at one of the Easter liturgies and taken home. Notes could be written for parents about the Eastertime blessing of homes with this water. (A simple rite for this will be found in *Catholic Household Blessings and Prayers,* page 153.)

Junior high
If it is the practice of the parish to confirm during the junior high years, then this season might be seen as the preparation (or follow-up) time each year. We will do well to understand confirmation in its original and most meaningful setting: the solemn anointing that follows on baptism (as done at the Vigil) and prepares for the fullness of initiation in the eucharist. This is one reason why children should be welcome at the liturgies of the Triduum, including the Vigil.

Liturgy Preparation
The description given here is meant for a Mass that would be celebrated several times, even weekly, during Eastertime. As during Lent, one element of the entrance rite is emphasized during this season and then not used during the rest of the year. Because the Mass is celebrated more frequently, the liturgy of the word is kept very simple.

The font brimming with water should have a central place and the entrance rites should lead to and take place around this font. Flowers can be placed near the font. As all move to the font, sing "You have put on Christ" (page 211) or simply have it played on an instrument. Standing alongside the font, the presider makes the sign of the cross and speaks the greeting. Introductory words should remind us of what happened in this font at the Vigil—and what happened at this font or another to each of the children and adults. The sprinkling can even be introduced with reminders of all that water does: quench our thirst, wake us up with the splash of a cold shower, cleanse us, bring life and growth to all crops. On some occasions the blessing prayer over the water can be used (from the sacramentary, for Eastertime). During the sprinkling that follows, the children sing "You have put on Christ." Another song for the sprinkling is "Lord Jesus, from your wounded side" (page 69). The words of both songs are rooted in the scriptures; teachers and homilists should find a time during the season to review these words with the children.

The liturgy of the word might take place right there around the font, followed by a procession to the altar for the eucharist. In any case, the entrance rites conclude with the opening prayer when the sprinkling is finished.

A single scripture reading from the gospel may be sufficient. The stories about Emmaus, doubting Thomas, Mary Magdalene and the gardener who was Jesus, the disciples' fishing trip and their breakfast with Jesus—all are worth telling year after year. The gospel on the Fourth Sunday of Easter is always of the Good Shepherd, and this also should be heard by the children during the week. In the week before Pentecost, the gospel might be of Jesus speaking of the Spirit that will come upon his disciples.

The Easter alleluia should be very special, perhaps heard only during this season (or, as suggested above, also on the feast of the Holy Cross). The Celtic alleluia (page 75) is a good choice for this, as is the alleluia from "O sons and daughters" (page 170). If there is a reading before the gospel, it could be followed by a psalm. Psalm 23 (two refrains, page 57 and page 58) or Psalm 114 or Psalm 118 (both on page 64) are good choices. Two or three of these could be learned and used here and at communion.

The homilist can find much to unfold by pondering the gospel that is read, the rites of initiation and the lives of the children. All of the psalm texts and song words are to be part of this ongoing Easter reflection with the children.

For the eucharistic prayer, the same acclamations used during Lent can be continued through Eastertime. This can give a sense for the unity of these seasons. Another possibility is the use of the third eucharistic prayer for Masses with children; this prayer includes special texts for use during Eastertime.

This season might be the one time of the year to make use of a different setting of the Lamb of God, thus marking the breaking of the bread in a special way. (The children should come, over the years, to know the beauty of the words, "they recognized him in the breaking of the bread.")

For communion songs, look always to those with refrains so that no books are needed except by the cantor or student choir. Possibilities include: "Now we remain" (page 160, with its refrain, "We hold the death of the Lord"), "Jubilate Deo" (page 147), Psalm 33 with its "Happy the people the Lord has chosen" refrain (page 59), the psalms mentioned above with the liturgy of the word, "Gift of finest wheat" (page 126), "I received the living God" (page 136). Several of these could be learned through the weeks of Eastertime. Likewise, several concluding songs could be learned and used: "The Lord, the Lord, the Lord is my shepherd" (page 194), "That Easter day with joy was bright" (page 192), "Sing with all the saints in glory" (page 184), "Ye watchers and ye holy ones" (page 210).

In the final weeks of Easter, the refrain "Veni Sancte Spiritus" (page 197) might be introduced either at communion or at the conclusion of the liturgy.

Ascension Day

This is a liturgy of the Easter season. Everything can be done as during the other liturgies of the season, except that the readings for Ascension should be used (at least the first reading and the gospel) and the song "Alleluia, sing to Jesus" (page 106). The words of this hymn are about the mystery of the ascension and, along with the scriptures, provide reflection for the homilist. The homilist could draw on these and emphasize our solidarity with Christ, our share in God's reign and our task in preparing for that reign. (Note that the paschal candle is *not* extinguished today but remains lighted and in place until the end of Eastertime on Pentecost.)

Because this is a Holy Day, the children may be celebrating the liturgy with part of the larger parish community. Prepare the liturgy so that both children and adults can fully participate. Neither group should feel like specators at the other group's liturgy.

Between Ascension and Pentecost, the daily prayer might include the song "O Holy Spirit, by whose breath" (page 169) or the "Veni Sancte Spiritus" (page 197) as a preparation for the feast of Pentecost.

In some years, this liturgy will be the time to mark the closing of the school year.

Prayer Service to End the School Year

It is right to gather in prayer on the last day of school. It is also right to keep it very brief. This could be based on the prayer from the beginning or ending of the day, with a special blessing at the end for protection and joy in the summer days.

Another form of the service would be the following:

Song from the year's liturgies, one that will be sung strongly

Reading from scripture (for example, Matthew 5:13–16, on being salt and light for the world)

Prayers of intercession for the school, the parish, teachers, administrators, helpers, students, as well as the needs of the world

Lord's Prayer, solemn blessing and dismissal

Closing hymn (e.g., "Let us walk in the light," page 152, or "Shalom," page 177)

Mass of the Holy Spirit

BACKGROUND

The church has a set of prayers (under Votive Masses in the Sacramentary) and scripture readings (taken from Pentecost or the liturgy for confirmation) for a Mass that calls upon the Holy Spirit to fill us and bless our work. Often this is used at the beginning of a new school year or at the time of graduation. It should not be confused with the feast of Pentecost, nor should it be used to have a "Pentecost liturgy" at the end of the school year. Pentecost is a Sunday. It concludes Eastertime. It should not be the name of any other day or liturgy.

This liturgy may be one that becomes a regular part of the school year, or it may be used only for some very special circumstances, or it may not be used at all.

CLASSROOM PREPARATION

The words to hymns and refrains as well as the scriptures for the Mass would be the subject of study and discussion in the classrooms. The scripture study should look also to places like 1 Corinthians 12 with its discussion of the gifts of the spirit in the community and the parts of the body, Numbers 11:25–29 for its story of how God's spirit is going to surprise us, the many places in the Hebrew Scriptures that refer to the spirit of God in telling of the prophets (Ezekiel 37, for example, where the spirit comes upon the dry bones). Talk about how the spirit of God is blowing around the world today and where we might see that spirit manifest in great or small ways. Talk about how we use the word "spirit" and how in the Bible it has roots in the word for "breath" and "wind" as in the very first lines of Genesis. The images from scripture of a dove and of fire may be helpful, but they are also incomplete. The short prayer to the Holy Spirit on page 219 of the *Hymnal* should be memorized even by the youngest students.

Explore the ways in which different gifts are manifest in the parish and in the school. This can be seen in different organizations and ministries and in the activity of individuals. Don't limit this activity to "churchy" things. Talk also of how most Catholics manifest the Holy Spirit in their work and family and community.

Preparation for this liturgy—as well as preparation for the Sunday celebration of Pentecost if this falls during the school year—is an excellent time to see the great diversity of the church around the world. Pictures of Catholics from every continent and many countries could be collected. Students and teachers also need a sense that we live in a time of movement from a largely European or European-controlled church to a truly catholic church in which the churches of Africa, Latin America and Asia—all with their own diversities—will all alike make up this church. This solidarity should find concrete expression in exchanges of letters, sending help to and asking for help from churches in other lands. Clergy and religious who have ministered in other countries could be invited to talk with the students and be present for the liturgy.

There are many dimensions to this liturgy, as there should be. One caution should be given. This liturgy should not be associated narrowly with confirmation. We receive the Holy Spirit in baptism. Confirmation is also part of our initiation and its scriptures and songs celebrate and pray for the Spirit. Avoid giving the impression that the Holy Spirit is somehow withheld until confirmation.

LITURGY PREPARATION

Red is a color associated with the Holy Spirit: fire from Pentecost and blood of the martyrs who were strengthened by the Spirit. Red clothing, red vestments, red banners in the procession, red ribbons from the processional cross: all are in place.

The order of the liturgy would follow the usual patterns established for the eucharist. See the "Index of Music" in this volume for appropriate songs and refrains. For scripture readings see the lectionary texts for Pentecost (including the Vigil of Pentecost) and confirmation. Psalm 104 (page 63) is appropriate.

Mass for the Patronal Feast

BACKGROUND

Every community should have a few days that are celebrated with traditions and enthusiasm that are unique just to this one place. For some parishes and schools, this will be the saint for whom the institution is named. Other places are named for one title or another of the Lord (e.g., Good Shepherd Parish) or for some mystery of the faith (Ascension Parish). On the appropriate feast day, a parish needs to celebrate its name and its work and its patron. The patronal feast of the parish could be a day for the children to host a liturgical celebration open to the whole parish. This liturgy would probably be celebrated in the evening so many could attend.

Such locally special days can come from other directions also: the patron of the religious order whose members serve the parish, the anniversary of the dedication of the church, the patron of the town or the feast special to one of the ethnic groups in the community. Even the name's day of the pastor or the principal might be worthy of celebration.

Much about the liturgy will depend on the origin of the celebration and on what customs or traditions may already be established and waiting for some fresh, enthusiastic participants. Whatever the occasion, the effect should be to grow in a sense of the heritage we have received—the faith itself and the good works of those who have gone before—and which we are to make lively in today's world before we in turn hand it on to those who follow us. In a way, all these feasts are celebrations of the communion of saints, but that communion made very local and real. Every community needs a day each year that is like a birthday for the individual: a day to celebrate what makes this place and community unique, blessed, challenged.

CLASSROOM PREPARATION

Much depends on the occasion. For some local feasts, it will be appropriate for the students—at their different levels—to learn about the local history and the ethnic traditions. Some of this can be simply the exploration of the buildings, statues, pictures and other artwork. Some of it might be in visits with the true elders of the community. Because the liturgy itself may involve the whole parish and not only the children, the children's part might be in the preparation of some music to be used in the liturgy or some art for the entranceway.

If it is a patron saint that is the focus, the children should be able each year to learn a little more about the saint's life. Exploring the history of the parish might be a task for older students: time line, important persons, struggles and divisions, successes. The students could visit the place where the parish records are kept to see the baptismal and other sacramental lists. Some looking into the future might also be part of this.

If special music is to be sung for the feast, this also will be part of the classroom preparation: study of the words and practice of the tune.

LITURGY PREPARATION

If appropriate, a statue or icon or other image of the saint or mystery can be given a place of importance (perhaps in the space that leads into the church or room for the liturgy). Several candles can be lighted around this image.

This liturgy would follow the usual pattern for the eucharist. On some occasions (for example, when the feast comes during Lent), a liturgy of the word may be a more appropriate form of celebration.

The *Hymnal* includes several songs in honor of the saints. These are listed in the "Index of Music" in the appendix of this book. Hymns from the ethnic tradition may be appropriate and important to the festival. The litany of saints, as suggested for November 1, and other music from All Saints Day may be in place.

The readings would be taken from the lectionary for the appropriate day. For some saints' feasts, a selection of texts will be found in the "common" texts (e.g., for martyrs, apostles).

CHAPTER SIX

Daily Prayer

The *Hymnal for Catholic Students* begins with an order of daily prayer in two parts: "Prayer to Begin the Day" and "Prayer to End the Day." Though the greater part of the *Hymnal* is given to the Mass and music for the Mass, the book is intended also for the classroom. In that setting, it offers these two times of prayer. They are based on the church's ancient way of praying in the morning and in the evening. The format can be adapted as needed for the age of the children and the daily schedule over the year. The intent is to have a stable order for daily prayer, one which the children come to know through the year and even from one year to the next. It leaves room for creativity and spontaneity while giving the children texts that can take much repetition and still show themselves full of meaning.

THE ORDER OF DAILY PRAYER

Both the morning and the afternoon prayer have this structure:

Beginning acclamation, with the sign of the cross
Glory be . . .
Morning hymn/Evening hymn
Psalmody
    Psalm 146/Psalm 121
    Psalm prayer
The Word of God
    Reading
    Silent reflection
    Canticle of Zachary/Canticle of Mary
Intercessions
    Prayers of intercession
    The Lord's Prayer
Concluding prayer
Blessing

This format allows for variations, but these should be done for a long period and not on a day to day basis. For example, the gospel canticle could be omitted. If both morning and afternoon prayer are done in the classroom, perhaps the reading of scripture and the intercessions could be omitted from one and the psalmody from the other. In the hymn, it could be the practice to sing only a single verse each day, but with a rotation by day or by week through the verses. When to sing anything is a problem, the hymn could be omitted and the psalm and canticle could be read in unison (perhaps alternating the verses, one side against the other). When singing comes easily, even the opening verse and the Glory Be can be chanted on a tone, as can the Lord's Prayer.

In general, a few moments of silence before beginning will help children and teacher make a transition into the prayer. During this time a candle can be lighted by one of the children. The candle's place would be beside the cross or icon that is a focus for these times of prayer.

Once begun, the familiar order of the prayer should flow from one element to the next, without hurry but also without long pauses except for a silent time of perhaps half a minute after the reading from scripture.

Once the format is adapted, there is the daily task of choosing a text from scripture. Two selections are given within the daily prayer and a number of others will be found in the final section of the book. It would be possible simply to alternate these through the days. However, with some planning a broader selection of scripture is possible. A good children's translation of the Bible could be used with the reading moving continuously from day to day through a given book of the Bible. The children's Bible will usually have less appropriate passages omitted, so it is possible to tackle some of the important books of the Hebrew Scripture including the stories of Genesis, Exodus, Samuel and Kings as well as the shorter books like Esther, Tobit and Ruth. The epistles of the Christian Scripture could be read in this same way. This would be interrupted, of course, during the seasons (Advent, Christmastime, Lent, Eastertime). Here it would be best to look at the daily readings in the lectionary and to select a few of these, dividing them into short passages where possible. Or one could choose to read continuously during these seasons also. The first chapter of Luke could be read in short sections during Advent, the second chapter during Christmastime, the gospels during Lent with Matthew in Cycle A, Mark in Cycle B, Luke in Cycle C (in each, selecting chapters appropriate to the age of the children), and during Eastertime chapters from Acts of the Apostles and Revelation.

The intercessions given need not be used every day. They are guides to the sorts of things we pray for daily. In some situations, the leader can prepare one or two intercessions and depend on others to mention additional needs. As early as possible, the students should be encouraged to mention their own prayers at this time. These can be specific and should always be brief and conclude with the words that lead to the response, "Lord, hear our prayer." Or it may become the practice to just mention prayers without any spoken response after each. The danger in spontaneous prayers is that the same people speak the same prayers day after day. This can be avoided to some extent if the teacher has the intercessions somewhere in mind through the day. Then if something appropriate to the community's prayer comes up in public or in private, the teacher can suggest to the student that this be prayed for with the class.

Two translations of the Lord's Prayer are given. The first is the one familiar to us. The second is a translation that has been in use for some years as a shared text among many churches. Catholics have not introduced it into the eucharistic liturgy, but it is often used in ecumenical gatherings. Though it may be confusing to younger children to be learning two translations, older students could come to know the ecumenical translation for the light it sheds on the meaning of the prayer.

The daily prayer would not change greatly from Ordinary Time to the seasons except as mentioned above for the scripture readings. It may be desirable to substitute a seasonal hymn for the morning or evening hymn. Thus, for example, different verses of "O come, O come, Emmanuel" could be sung on the days of Advent.

Except for the hymn and the canticle, the children should not need the books for daily prayer once they have learned the few simple responses and the psalm refrain. Even the verses of the hymn and canticle will be memorized in a short while. Children in first grade who are not reading yet can still be introduced to this format of daily prayer, learning by heart one verse of the morning hymn and one verse of the evening hymn.

POSTURES AND GESTURES IN DAILY PRAYER

An order for posture and gestures during daily prayer should be established at the beginning of the school year. Generally, the children will stand at the beginning, sit for the psalmody and the scripture, stand again for the intercessions and until the conclusion.

The sign of the cross at the beginning can be the large sign of the cross made on forehead, heart and shoulders, but it can also be the small sign of the cross made with the thumb on the lips. This latter is especially appropriate for morning prayer ("O Lord, open my lips"). The church has also had a practice of making the sign of the cross during the first words of the canticles of Zachary and Mary. And the sign of the cross should be made again with the blessing that concludes the prayer.

When the students are not holding their books, it may be possible to suggest that they take postures that have been traditional in the church during times of prayer. During the prayers of intercession the hands can be folded. During the Lord's Prayer, hands and arms can be somewhat extended.

Daily prayer is the time when we learn about the pace of prayer and about silence within public prayer. The silent time after the scripture reading has been mentioned. This can be presented as a time to let the words—all of them or just one of them or a single phrase—resound in one's mind and heart. A short silence may also be in place before the concluding prayer, but if this is done it should be introduced with the invitation, "Let us pray," then the silence.

Sometimes it is possible to bring other gestures into these prayers. Holy water is appropriate at the beginning of morning prayer or the end of afternoon prayer. If the group is small, each person can take holy water for the sign of the cross. If the group is large, the teacher can sprinkle them with holy water at the conclusion of afternoon prayer. This gesture would be especially appropriate during all the days of Eastertime. (If holy water is used all through the year, it might be put aside during Lent.) The container for the holy water should be something worthy; it could have a place of honor near the door to the room.

On some special feast days, incense could be burned during the afternoon prayer. The coals could be prepared in a censer or other suitable (and safe) vessel and lighted well before the prayer begins. Like the candle, the incense would be placed near the cross or icon. Incense can be added at the beginning of the prayer and again just before the intercessions. At the latter time, the leader could first place a few grains of incense on the coals, then introduce the intercessions with the words: "My prayers rise like incense." With a small group, it can be the practice for individual children to come forward during the intercessions to add a grain or two of incense to the coals.

Another variation in the order of service might be the specific mention of Fridays. In their pastoral letter *The Challenge of Peace,* the United States bishops ask that Catholics fast and do penance and works of charity on Fridays for the cause of peace. This invitation can be extended to the children and adults of the community. It can then become a part of prayer on each Friday. A prayer is suggested in *Catholic Household Blessings and Prayers,* page 63 and pages 193–94.

LEADERS OF PRAYER

At daily prayer in the classroom children can experience the same dynamics between the assembly and its ministers that are at work at the eucharistic liturgy. They can learn that those who minister are first of all part of the assembly and that to be a minister is to take on a responsibility. It should also become clear in a very natural way that some are suited for one ministry and some for another. This does not mean that the task of reading the scripture, for example, should not be given to each person in turn, but the ideal would be a situation where it comes about that some are lectors, some musicians and so on.

Except with the younger children, the leader should be one of the students. Each person who is willing should take this role for several days in succession. Ordinarily, the leader's position would be in front of the others, but this would depend on the arrangement of the room. For a prayer as simple and as frequent as this, the leader could well remain at his or her regular place in the room. In practicing with persons who are to take the role of leader, the teacher should work for clarity in speech and for the right pace both in speaking words and in the flow from one part of the service to the next.

The role of lector requires that a person be able to read clearly and with understanding and be heard by all. The book from which the lector reads should have a place of honor in the room. When the time comes for the reading, the lector takes the book and stands facing the other children. The book will normally be held during the reading. The lector would usually remain in position during the silence that follows the "Thanks be to God." Then the book is returned to its place as the children stand for the intercessions.

With older children, it may be possible to have leaders of song. Their primary role would be to sing the verses of the psalm (otherwise these may be read by the one who is lector for the week, pausing after each verse for the refrain to be sung).

The classroom teacher's role, when these forms of prayer are first introduced, is to work with other teachers early in the year to discover how to guide the children through the prayer in the first few days and weeks. The teacher should also, from time to time, explore with the children the various words and gestures that make up these prayers. The images of the hymns and canticles and psalms should be points of reference that can come up in dozens of ways through the school year. The readings from scripture also begin to provide teacher and student with the church's most basic vocabulary. Over the years, these songs and prayers and scriptures become a strong foundation for the faith of the adolescent and adult.

APPENDIX

The Directory for Masses with Children

Background of the Directory

The importance of this 1973 document from the Roman Congregation for Divine Worship has yet to be fully realized. The Introduction and the first chapter are especially important for the remarkable approach they take to the place of ritual in the life of the family and the local church. Nearly every sentence here is worth reflection and discussion. These insights have many and sometimes subtle applications to school Masses and other children's liturgies.

Chapters 2 and 3 take us into the ministries and order of the Mass. Realism and humor are not lacking (as in number 16: "Infants who as yet are unable or unwilling [emphasis added] to take part in the Mass . . ."). What comes through with wonderful clarity is the responsibility of those who minister at the liturgy and those who prepare the liturgy for children. These people must love the liturgy, must know its ways, must sense that they are charged to help a new generation make its own the ways of Catholic worship.

This document was published before the three eucharistic prayers for Masses with children were approved (as is clear from the last paragraph of number 52). Those eucharistic prayers are themselves a partial expression of the goals sought by this Directory.

Introduction

1   The Church must show special concern for baptized children who have yet to be fully initiated through the sacraments of confirmation and eucharist as well as for children who have only recently been admitted to holy communion. Today the circumstances in which children grow up are not favorable to their spiritual progress.[1] In addition parents sometimes scarcely fulfill the obligations they

accepted at the baptism of their children to bring them up as Christians.

2 In the upbringing of children in the Church a special difficulty arises from the fact that liturgical celebrations, especially the eucharist, cannot fully exercise their inherent pedagogical force upon children.[2] Although the vernacular may now be used at Mass, still the words and signs have not been sufficiently adapted to the capacity of children.

In fact, even in daily life children do not always understand all their experiences with adults but rather may find them boring. It cannot therefore be expected of the liturgy that everything must always be intelligible to them. Nonetheless, we may fear spiritual harm if over the years children repeatedly experience in the Church things that are barely comprehensible: recent psychological study has established how profoundly children are formed by the religious experience of infancy and early childhood, because of the special religious receptivity proper to those years.[3]

3 The Church follows its Master, who "put his arms around the children . . . and blessed them" (Mark 10:16). It cannot leave children in the condition described. Vatican Council II had spoken in the *Constitution on the Liturgy* about the need of liturgical adaptation for various groups.[4] Soon afterwards, especially in the first Synod of Bishops held in Rome in 1967, the Church began to consider how participation by children could be easier. On the occasion of the Synod, the President of the Consilium for the Implementation of the *Constitution on the Liturgy* said explicitly that it could not be a matter of "creating some entirely special rite but rather of retaining, shortening, or omitting some elements or of making a better selection of texts."[5]

4 All the details of eucharistic celebration with a congregation were determined in the General Instruction of the revised Roman Missal published in 1969. Then this Congregation began to prepare a special Directory for Masses with Children, as a supplement to the General Instruction. This was done in response to repeated petitions from the entire Catholic world and with the cooperation of men and women specialists from almost every nation.

5 Like the *General Instruction of the Roman Missal*, this Directory reserves some adaptations to the conference of bishops or to individual bishops.[6]

Some adaptations of the Mass may be necessary for children in a given country but cannot be included in a general directory. In accord with the *Constitution on the Liturgy* art. 40, the conferences of bishops are to propose such adaptations to the Apostolic See for introduction into the liturgy with its consent.

6   The Directory is concerned with children who have not yet entered the period of preadolescence. It does not speak directly of children who are physically or mentally handicapped, because a broader adaptation is sometimes necessary for them.[7] Nevertheless, the following norms may also be applied to the handicapped, with the necessary changes.

7   The first chapter of the Directory (nos. 8–15) gives a kind of foundation by considering the different ways in which children are introduced to the eucharistic liturgy. The second chapter briefly treats Masses with adults in which children also take part (nos. 16–19). Finally, the third chapter (nos. 20–54) treats at greater length Masses with children in which only some adults take part.

Chapter I

THE INTRODUCTION OF CHILDREN TO THE EUCHARISTIC CELEBRATION

8   A fully Christian life is inconceivable without participation in the liturgical services in which the faithful, gathered into a single assembly, celebrate the paschal mystery. Therefore, the religious initiation of children must be in harmony with this purpose.[8] The Church baptizes children and therefore, relying on the gifts conferred by this sacrament, it must be concerned that once baptized they grow in communion with Christ and each other. The sign and pledge of that communion is participation in the eucharistic table, for which children are being prepared or led to a deeper realization of its meaning. This liturgical and eucharistic formation may not be separated from their general education, both human and Christian; indeed it would be harmful if their liturgical formation lacked such a basis.

9   For this reason all who have a part in the formation of children should consult and work together toward one objective: that even if children already have some feeling for God and the things of God, they may also experience in proportion to their age and personal development the human values that are present in the eucharistic celebration. These values include the community activity, exchange of greetings, capacity to listen and to seek and grant pardon,

expression of gratitude, experience of symbolic actions, a meal of friendship, and festive celebration.[9]

Eucharistic catechesis, dealt with in no. 12, should develop such human values. Then, depending on their age and their psychological and social situation, children will gradually open their minds to the perception of Christian values and the celebration of the mystery of Christ.[10]

10   The Christian family has the greatest role in instilling these Christian and human values.[11] Thus Christian education, provided by parents and other educators, should be strongly encouraged in relation to the liturgical formation of children as well.

By reason of the duty in conscience freely accepted at the baptism of their children, parents are bound to teach them gradually how to pray. This they do by praying with them each day and by introducing them to prayers said privately.[12] If children, prepared in this way even from their early years, take part in the Mass with their family when they wish, they will easily begin to sing and to pray in the liturgical community and indeed will already have some initial idea of the eucharistic mystery.

If the parents are weak in faith but still wish their children to receive Christian formation, they should be urged at least to communicate to their children the human values mentioned already, and when the occasion arises, to participate in meetings of parents and in noneucharistic celebrations held with children.

11   The Christian communities to which the individual families belong or in which the children live also have a responsibility toward children baptized in the Church. By giving witness to the Gospel, living communal charity, and actively celebrating the mysteries of Christ, the Christian community is an excellent school of Christian and liturgical formation for the children who live in it.

Within the Christian community, godparents or other persons noted for their dedicated service can, out of apostolic zeal, contribute greatly to the necessary catechesis in the case of families that fail in their obligation toward the children's Christian upbringing.

Preschool programs, Catholic schools, and various kinds of associations for children serve these same ends in a special way.

12   Even in the case of children, the liturgy itself always exerts its own inherent power to instruct.[13] Yet within religious-education programs in the schools and parishes the necessary importance should be given to catechesis on the Mass.[14] This catechesis should be directed to the child's active, conscious, and authentic

participation.[15] "Suited to children's age and capabilities, it should, by means of the main rites and prayers of the Mass, aim at conveying its meaning, including what relates to taking part in the Church's life."[16] This is especially true of the text of the eucharistic prayer and of the acclamation by which the children take part in this prayer.

The catechesis preparing children for first communion calls for special mention. In it they should learn not only the truths of faith regarding the eucharist but also how from first communion on—after being prepared according to their capacity by penance—they can as full members of Christ's Body take part actively with the people of God in the eucharist, sharing in the Lord's table and the community of their brothers and sisters.

13 Various kinds of celebrations may also play a major role in the liturgical formation of children and in their preparation for the Church's liturgical life. By the very fact of such celebrations children easily come to appreciate some liturgical elements, for example, greetings, silence, and common praise (especially when this is sung together). But care must be taken that the instructive element does not become dominant in these celebrations.

14 Depending on the capacity of the children, the word of God should have a greater and greater place in these celebrations. In fact, as the children's spiritual capacity develops, celebrations of the word of God in the strict sense should be held frequently, especially during Advent and Lent.[17] These will help greatly to develop in the children an appreciation of the word of God.

15 While all that has been said remains true, the final purpose of all liturgical and eucharistic formation must be a greater and greater conformity to the Gospel in the daily life of the children.

Chapter II

MASSES WITH ADULTS IN WHICH CHILDREN ALSO PARTICIPATE

16 In many places parish Masses are celebrated, especially on Sundays and holy days, at which a good many children take part along with the large number of adults. On such occasions the witness of adult believers can have a great effect upon the children. Adults can in turn benefit spiritually from experiencing the part that the children have within the Christian community. The Christian spirit of the family is greatly fostered when children take part in these Masses together with their parents and other family members.

Infants who as yet are unable or unwilling to take part in the Mass may be brought in at the end of Mass to be blessed together with the rest of the community. This may be done, for example, if parish helpers have been taking care of them in a separate area.

17   Nevertheless, in Masses of this kind it is necessary to take great care that the children present do not feel neglected because of their inability to participate or to understand what happens and what is proclaimed in the celebration. Some account should be taken of their presence: for example, by speaking to them directly in the introductory comments (as at the beginning and the end of Mass) and at some point in the homily.

Sometimes, moreover, if the place itself and the nature of the community permit, it will be appropriate to celebrate the liturgy of the word, including a homily, with the children in a separate, but not too distant, room. Then, before the eucharistic liturgy begins, the children are led to the place where the adults have meanwhile celebrated their own liturgy of the word.

18   It may also be very helpful to give some tasks to the children. They may, for example, bring forward the gifts or perform one or other of the songs of the Mass.

19   If the number of children is large, it may at times be suitable to plan the Mass so that it corresponds more closely to the needs of the children. In this case the homily should be directed to them but in such a way that adults may also benefit from it. Wherever the bishop permits, in addition to the adaptations already provided in the Order of Mass, one or other of the particular adaptations described later in the Directory may be employed in a Mass celebrated with adults in which children also participate.

Chapter III

MASSES WITH CHILDREN IN WHICH
ONLY A FEW ADULTS PARTICIPATE

20   In addition to the Masses in which children take part with their parents and other family members (which are not always possible everywhere), Masses with children in which only a few adults take part are recommended, especially during the week. From the beginning of the liturgical reform it has been clear to everyone that some adaptations are necessary in these masses.[18]

Such adaptations, but only those of a more general kind, will be considered later (nos. 38–54).

21   It is always necessary to keep in mind that these eucharistic celebrations must lead children toward the celebration of Mass with adults, especially the Masses at which the Christian community must come together on Sundays.[19] Thus, apart from adaptations that are necessary because of the children's age, the result should not be entirely special rites, markedly different from the Order of Mass celebrated with a congregation.[20] The purpose of the various elements should always correspond with what is said in the *General Instruction of the Roman Missal* on individual points, even if at times for pastoral reasons an absolute *identity* cannot be insisted upon.

OFFICES AND MINISTRIES IN THE CELEBRATION

22   The principles of active and conscious participation are in a sense even more significant for Masses celebrated with children. Every effort should therefore be made to increase this participation and to make it more intense. For this reason as many children as possible should have special parts in the celebration: for example, preparing the place and the altar (see no. 29), acting as cantor (see no. 24), singing in a choir, playing musical instruments (see no. 32), proclaiming the readings (see nos. 24 and 27), responding during the homily (see no. 48), reciting the intentions of the general intercessions, bringing the gifts to the altar, and performing similar activities in accord with the usage of various peoples (see no. 34).

To encourage participation, it will sometimes be helpful to have several additions, for example, the insertion of motives for giving thanks before the priest begins the dialogue of the preface.

In all this, it should be kept in mind that external activities will be fruitless and even harmful if they do not serve the internal participation of the children. Thus religious silence has its importance even in Masses with children (see no. 37). The children should not be allowed to forget that all the forms of participation reach their high point in eucharistic communion, when the body and blood of Christ are received as spiritual nourishment.[21]

23   It is the responsibility of the priest who celebrates with children to make the celebration festive, familial, and meditative.[22] Even more than in Masses with adults, the priest is the one to create this kind of attitude, which depends on his personal preparation and his manner of acting and speaking with others.

The priest should be concerned above all about the dignity, clarity, and simplicity of his actions and gestures. In speaking to the children he should express himself so that he will be easily understood, while avoiding any childish style of speech.

The free use of introductory comments[23] will lead children to a genuine liturgical participation, but these should be more than mere explanatory remarks.

It will help him to reach the hearts of the children if the priest sometimes expresses the invitations in his own words, for example, at the penitential rite, the prayer over the gifts, the Lord's Prayer, the sign of peace, and communion.

24 Since the eucharist is always the action of the entire ecclesial community, the participation of at least some adults is desirable. These should be present not as monitors but as participants, praying with the children and helping them to the extent necessary.

With the consent of the pastor or rector of the church, one of the adults may speak to the children after the gospel, especially if the priest finds it difficult to adapt himself to the mentality of children. In this matter the norms soon to be issued by the Congregation for the Clergy should be observed.

Even in Masses with children attention is to be paid to the diversity of ministries so that the Mass may stand out clearly as the celebration of a community.[24] For example, readers and cantors, whether children or adults, should be employed. In this way a variety of voices will keep the children from becoming bored.

PLACE AND TIME OF CELEBRATION

25 The primary place for the eucharistic celebration for children is the church. Within the church, however, a space should be carefully chosen if available, that will be suited to the number of participants. It should be a place where the children can act with a feeling of ease according to the requirements of a living liturgy that is suited to their age.

If the church does not satisfy these demands, it will sometimes be suitable to celebrate the eucharist with children outside a place of worship. But in that case the place chosen should be appropriate and worthy of the celebration.[25]

26 The time of day chosen for Masses with children should correspond to the circumstances of their lives so that they may be most open to hearing the word of God and to celebrating the eucharist.

27 Weekday Mass in which children participate can certainly be celebrated with greater effect and less danger of boredom if it does not take place every day (for example, in boarding schools). Moreover, preparation can be more careful if there is a longer interval between diverse celebrations.

Sometimes it will be preferable to have common prayer, to which the children may contribute spontaneously, or else a common meditation, or a celebration of the word of God. These are ways of continuing the eucharistic celebrations already held and of leading to a deeper participation in subsequent celebrations.

28   When the number of children who celebrate the eucharist together is very great, attentive and conscious participation becomes more difficult. Therefore, if possible, several groups should be formed; these should not be set up rigidly according to age but with regard for the children's progress in religious formation and catechetical preparation.

During the week such groups may be invited to the sacrifice of the Mass on different days.

PREPARATION FOR THE CELEBRATION

29   Each eucharistic celebration with children should be carefully prepared beforehand, especially with regard to the prayers, songs, readings, and intentions of the general intercessions. This should be done in discussion with the adults and with the children who will have a special ministry in these Masses. If possible, some of the children should take part in preparing and ornamenting the place of celebration and preparing the chalice with the paten and the cruets. Presupposing the appropriate internal participation, such activity will help to develop the spirit of community celebration.

SINGING AND MUSIC

30   Singing must be given great importance in all celebrations, but it is to be especially encouraged in every way for Masses celebrated with children, in view of their special affinity for music.[26] The culture of various peoples and the capabilities of the children present should be taken into account.

If possible, the acclamations should be sung by the children rather than recited, especially the acclamations that form part of the eucharistic prayer.

31   To facilitate the children's participation in singing the Gloria, Credo, Sanctus, and Agnus Dei, it is permissible to use with the melodies appropriate vernacular texts, accepted by competent authority, even if these do not correspond exactly to the liturgical texts.[27]

32   The use of "musical instruments can add a great deal" in Masses with children, especially if they are played by the children themselves.[28] The playing of instruments will help to sustain the

singing or to encourage the reflection of the children; sometimes in their own fashion instruments express festive joy and praise of God.

Care should always be taken, however, that the musical accompaniment does not overpower the singing or become a distraction rather than a help to the children. Music should correspond to the purpose intended for the different periods at which it is played during the Mass.

With these precautions and with due and special discretion, recorded music may also be used in Masses with children, in accord with norms established by the conferences of bishops.

GESTURES

33   In view of the nature of the liturgy as an activity of the entire person and in view of the psychology of children, participation by means of gestures and posture should be strongly encouraged in Masses with children, with due regard for age and local customs. Much depends not only on the actions of the priest,[29] but also on the manner in which the children conduct themselves as a community.

If, in accord with the norms of the *General Instruction of the Roman Missal*,[30] a conference of bishops adapts the congregation's actions at Mass to the mentality of a people, it should take the special condition of children into account or should decide on adaptations that are for children only.

34   Among the actions that are considered under this heading, processions and other activities that involve physical participation deserve special mention.

The children's entering in procession with the priest can serve to help them to experience a sense of the communion that is thus being created.[31] The participation of at least some children in the procession with the Book of the Gospels makes clear the presence of Christ announcing the word to his people. The procession of children with the chalice and the gifts expresses more clearly the value and meaning of the preparation of the gifts. The communion procession, if properly arranged, helps greatly to develop the children's devotion.

VISUAL ELEMENTS

35   The liturgy of the Mass contains many visual elements and these should be given great prominence with children. This is especially true of the particular visual elements in the course of the liturgical year, for example, the veneration of the cross, the Easter candle, the

lights on the feast of the Presentation of the Lord, and the variety of colors and liturgical appointments.

In addition to the visual elements that belong to the celebration and to the place of celebration, it is appropriate to introduce other elements that will permit children to perceive visually the wonderful works of God in creation and redemption and thus support their prayer. The liturgy should never appear as something dry and merely intellectual.

36   For the same reason, the use of artwork prepared by the children themselves may be useful, for example, as illustrations of a homily, as visual expressions of the intentions of the general intercessions, or as inspirations to reflection.

SILENCE

37   Even in Masses with children "silence should be observed at the designated times as part of the celebration"[32] lest too great a place be given to external action. In their own way children are genuinely capable of reflection. They need some guidance, however, so that they will learn how, in keeping with the different moments of the Mass (for example, after the homily or after communion[33]), to recollect themselves, meditate briefly, or praise God and pray to him in their hearts.[34]

Besides this, with even greater care than in Masses with adults, the liturgical texts should be proclaimed intelligibly and unhurriedly, with the necessary pauses.

PARTS OF THE MASS

38   The general structure of the Mass, which "is made up as it were of the liturgy of the word and the liturgy of the eucharist," should always be maintained, as should certain rites to open and conclude the celebration.[35] Within individual parts of the celebration, the adaptations that follow seem necessary if children are truly to experience in their own way and according to the psychological patterns of childhood, "the mystery of faith . . . by means of rites and prayers."[36]

39   Some rites and texts should never be adapted for children lest the difference between Masses with children and the Masses with adults become too pronounced.[37] These are "the acclamations and the responses to the priest's greeting,"[38] the Lord's Prayer, and the Trinitarian formulary at the end of the blessing with which the priest concludes the Mass. It is urged, moreover, that children

should become accustomed to the Nicene Creed little by little, the right to use the Apostles' Creed indicated in no. 49 remaining intact.

A. Introductory Rite

40 The introductory rite of Mass has the purpose "that the faithful coming together take on the form of a community and prepare themselves to listen to God's word and celebrate the eucharist properly."[39] Therefore every effort should be made to create this disposition in the children and not to jeopardize it by any excess of rites in this part of Mass.

It is sometimes proper to omit one or other element of the introductory rite or perhaps to expand one of the elements. There should always be at least some introductory element, which is completed by the opening prayer. In choosing individual elements, care should be taken that each one be used from time to time and that none be entirely neglected.

B. Reading and Explanation of the Word of God

41 Since readings taken from holy Scripture "form the main part of the liturgy of the word,"[40] even in Masses with children biblical reading should never be omitted.

42 With regard to the number of readings on Sundays and holy days, the decrees of the conferences of bishops are to be observed. If three or even two readings appointed on Sundays or weekdays can be understood by children only with difficulty, it is permissible to read two or only one of them, but the reading of the gospel should never be omitted.

43 If all the readings assigned to the day seem to be unsuited to the capacity of the children, it is permissible to choose readings or a reading either from the Lectionary of the Roman Missal or directly from the Bible, but taking into account the liturgical seasons. It is recommended, moreover, that the individual conferences of bishops see to the composition of lectionaries for Masses with children.

If, because of the limited capabilities of the children, it seems necessary to omit one or other verse of a biblical reading, this should be done cautiously and in such a way "that the meaning of the text or the intent and, as it were, style of the Scriptures are not distorted."[41]

44 In the choice of readings the criterion to be followed is the quality rather than the quantity of the texts from the Scriptures. A shorter reading is not as such always more suited to children than a

lengthy reading. Everything depends on the spiritual advantage that the reading can bring to the children.

45   In the biblical texts "God is speaking to his people . . . and Christ is present to the faithful through his own word."[42] Paraphrases of Scripture should therefore be avoided. On the other hand, the use of translations that may already exist for the catechesis of children and that are accepted by the competent authority is recommended.

46   Verses of psalms, carefully selected in accord with the understanding of children, or singing in the form of psalmody or the Alleluia with a simple verse should be sung between the readings. The children should always have a part in this singing, but sometimes a reflective silence may be substituted for the singing.

 If only a single reading is chosen, the singing may follow the homily.

47   All the elements that will help explain the readings should be given great consideration so that the children may make the biblical readings their own and may come more and more to appreciate the value of God's word.

 Among such elements are the introductory comments that may precede the readings[43] and that by explaining the context or by introducing the text itself help the children to listen better and more fruitfully. The interpretation and explanation of the readings from the Scriptures in the Mass on a saint's day may include an account of the saint's life, not only in the homily but even before the readings in the form of an introduction.

 When the text of the readings lends itself to this, it may be helpful to have the children read it with parts distributed among them, as is provided for the reading of the Lord's passion during Holy Week.

48   The homily explaining the word of God should be given great prominence in all Masses with children. Sometimes the homily intended for children should become a dialogue with them, unless it is preferred that they should listen in silence.

49   If the profession of faith occurs at the end of the liturgy of the word, the Apostle's Creed may be used with children, especially because it is part of their catechetical formation.

C. Presidential Prayers

50   The priest is permitted to choose from the Roman Missal texts of presidential prayers more suited to children, so that he may truly

associate the children with himself. But he is to take into account the liturgical season.

51   Since these prayers were composed for adult Christians, however, the principle simply of choosing from among them does not serve the purpose of having the children regard the prayers as an expression of their own life and religious experience.[44] If this is the case, the text of prayers of the Roman Missal may be adapted to the needs of children, but this should be done in such a way that, preserving the purpose of the prayer and to some extent its substance as well, the priest avoids anything that is foreign to the literary genre of a presidential prayer, such as moral exhortations or a childish manner of speech.

52   The eucharistic prayer is of the greatest importance in the eucharist celebrated with children because it is the high point of the entire celebration.[45] Much depends on the manner in which the priest proclaims this prayer[46] and on the way the children take part by listening and making their acclamations.

      The disposition of mind required for this central part of the celebration and the calm and reverence with which everything is done must make the children as attentive as possible. Their attention should be on the real presence of Christ on the altar under the elements of bread and wine, on his offering, on the thanksgiving through him and with him and in him, and on the Church's offering, which is made during the prayer and by which the faithful offer themselves and their lives with Christ to the eternal Father in the Holy Spirit.

      For the present, the four eucharistic prayers approved by the supreme authority for Masses with adults and introduced into liturgical use are to be employed until the Apostolic See makes other provision for Masses with children.

D. Rites before Communion

53   When the eucharistic prayer has ended, the Lord's Prayer, the breaking of bread, and the invitation to communion should always follow,[47] that is, the elements that have the principal significance in the structure of this part of the Mass.

E. Communion and the Following Rites

54   Everything should be done so that the children who are properly disposed and who have already been admitted to the eucharist may go to the holy table calmly and with recollection and thus take part fully in the eucharistic mystery. If possible, there should be singing, suited to the children, during the communion procession.[48]

The comments that precede the final blessing[49] are important in Masses with children. Before they are dismissed they need some repetition and application of what they have heard, but this should be done in a very few words. In particular, this is the appropriate time to express the connection between the liturgy and life.

At least sometimes, depending on the liturgical seasons and different occasions in the children's life, the priest should use more expanded forms of blessing, but at the end should always retain the Trinitarian formulary with the sign of the cross.[50]

55 The contents of the Directory have as their purpose to help children readily and joyfully to encounter Christ together in the eucharistic celebration and to stand with him in the presence of the Father.[51] If they are formed by conscious and active participation in the eucharistic sacrifice and meal, they should learn day by day, at home and away from home, to proclaim Christ to others among their family and among their peers, by living the "faith that works through love" (Galatians 5:6).

This Directory was prepared by the Congregation for Divine Worship. On 22 October 1973, Pope Paul VI approved and confirmed it and ordered that it be published.

Notes
1. See GCD 5.
2. See CSL 33.
3. See GCD 78.
4. See CSL 38; also AP.
5. First Synod of Bishops, Liturgy: *Notitiae* 3 (1967) 368.
6. See DMC 19, 32, 33.
7. See Order of Mass with children who are deafmutes for German-speaking countries, confirmed 26 June 1970 by CDW (prot. no. 1546/70).
8. See CSL 14, 19.
9. See GCD 25.
10. See Vatican Council II, Declaration on Christian Education, *Gravissimum educationis*, no. 2.
11. See *Ibid.*, 3.
12. See GCD 78.
13. See CSL 33.
14. See EM 14.
15. See GCD 25.
16. See EM 14; GCD 57.
17. See CSL 35, 4.

18. See DMC 3.
19. See CSL 42, 106.
20. See first Synod of Bishops, Liturgy: *Notitiae* 3 (1967) 368.
21. See GI 56.
22. See DMC 37.
23. See GI 11.
24. See CL 28.
25. See GI 253.
26. See GI 19.
27. See MS 55.
28. *Ibid.*, 62.
29. See DMC 23.
30. See GI 21.
31. See GI 24.
32. GI 23.
33. See EM 38.
34. See GI 23.
35. GI 8.
36. CSL 48.
37. See DMC 21.
38. GI 15.
39. GI 24.
40. GI 33.
41. Lectionary for Mass: Introduction, 1969 edition, no. 7d.
42. GI 33.
43. See GI 11.
44. See Consilium for the Implementation of the Constitution on the Sacred Liturgy, instruction on translations of liturgical texts for celebrations with a congregation, 25 Jan 1969, no. 20: *Notitiae* 5 (1969) 7.
45. GI 54.
46. See DMC 23, 37.
47. See DMC 23.
48. See MS 32.
49. See GI 11.
50. See DMC 39.
51. See Eucharistic prayer II.

Basics of Singing for the Classroom Teacher

In schools without music programs, the classroom teacher is often the only resource for learning music to be used in liturgy and for developing the basic vocal quality produced by the children in singing. The purpose here is to offer the busy classroom teacher, armed with basic piano skills or pitch pipe or reasonably pleasant voice, a few hints to make singing a beneficial and rewarding experience for children.

In our culture there are often misconceptions about how children should sound when singing: loud, enthusiastic sounds in low range are usually considered normal and acceptable, even when raucous, out of tune and possibly injurious to vocal health. Until recently, television has reinforced this popular image of children singing. But it seems that advertisers and producers have begun to present a quite different aural image of children's voices: high, light, clear, flute-like tone, well produced and in tune. Television has somehow discovered that beautiful singing by children is more ear-catching and convincing than raucous singing. Beauty sells the message!

Apart from the question of *what* is sung at children's liturgies, it is equally important to ask *how* it is sung. Our objective should be to encourage and produce the most beautiful singing tone possible, both for the lasting benefit of the children themselves and for their enriched participation in the liturgy.

1. Singing is sustained (slowed) speech, the result of prolonging vowels on specific pitches during the gradual, controlled exhaling of air from the lungs. Good breathing and healthy vocal mechanism are both needed to achieve proper singing. Natural deep breathing required for sustaining tone can be developed by encouraging children to inhale as deeply as possible, expanding the lower rib cage from the diaphragm (muscles) below the lungs.

Shoulders should always be kept down and relaxed when taking deep breaths. An exercise or game can be made of this by counting on one pitch, such as G or A above middle C: Ask the children to *inhale deeply* (expanding lower rib cage and keeping shoulders down), to *hold the air* briefly, and then to *exhale slowly* while singing numbers *one through ten, one through fifteen, one through twenty.* The numbers should be sung slowly, quietly, evenly. Each repeat of this exercise should be raised in pitch by one half-step (G, G#, A, A#, etc.). Children will always enjoy such an increasing challenge and will become competitive when this deep breathing needed for singing is compared to that used in swimming.

2. It is no secret that most children are skilled imitators. Placing the best singers behind or in the middle of other students will quicken vocal results.

3. The natural voice of children is high and light, the so-called "head voice." This upper voice can usually be discovered by asking children to imitate the sound of a police siren: the sound of "woo," swooping up to a high point, holding there briefly, and then falling in pitch. Repeating this a few times and sustaining the highest sound longer each time will usually reveal the natural high treble range of children's voices.

4. The single most important element in developing the upper vocal register is practicing *downward scales quietly.* Starting on a comfortable pitch (C above middle C), sing slowly and softly down the bottom half of the major scale (5-4-3-2-1 or sol-fa-me-re-do). Either scale numbers or solfège names may be used at first. Vocal results will increase when this little exercise is practiced with pure vowels, preceded by a consonant: loo, moo, foo, poo or koo. Use of the pure "oo" vowel should produce nearly automatic, effortless sounds in the head voices of children. Other useful pure vowels for exercise are *oh* and *ah*, always preceded by consonants as above. Each repeat of the descending should begin on a higher pitch (C, C#, D, D#, E, F). With a slow and even pace, the tones should be sung short and detached in one exercise, smooth and connected in the next. At all times, the sound should be quiet and beautiful, never forced.

5. A practical exercise is to extract a single phrase containing downward motion from a song or acclamation being learned. Practice this fragment first with words, then without, substituting open vowel sounds that are preceded by consonants, as indicated above. Repeating the phrase, always beginning on a

higher pitch, will reinforce the learning of the complete melody later and will develop the overtones of the upper vocal registers. Quiet humming can also be a useful exercise for children, but special care must be taken that lips and teeth are not tightly shut. Gentle humming on N (rather than M), with lips and teeth somewhat apart, will contribute to a good, effortless vocal sound.

6. At school liturgies, when few adults are likely to be present, it is always helpful to ask the organist or pianist to transpose printed hymns and acclamations upward one or two steps to favor correct head voice singing by children. (Most hymnals and other publications print music in keys designed for average adults rather than higher keys suited to children's voices.) Singing in generally higher keys allows the children to produce greater sonority, overcoming some of the acoustical difficulties built into most of our churches.

7. When the practice of deep breathing and soft, downward scales improve the quality and range of singing tone, it will be useful to teach the complete major scale at least, using either numbers (one–two–three–four–five–six–seven–eight) or solfège names (do–re–mi–fa–sol–la–ti–do). This will open the way to using and naming melodic intervals: one–five or do–sol. A well-known song from *The Sound of Music* will be of some help in teaching children this basic musical tool.

8. When teaching new hymns, acclamations or other songs, it is often helpful to separate melodic, rhythmic and textual problems. Simply speaking texts in rhythm, clapping difficult rhythms and vocalizing melodies on pure vowels substituted for texts will contribute thoroughness and fun to the process of both learning music and singing it well.

9. Children are naturally good singers. Frequent short sessions in a relaxed, good-humored atmosphere will reinforce the idea that good singing can be enjoyable and challenging. The natural voice of children is in the high, clear, light treble register. It is the health and beauty of this soaring treble sound that needs to be developed and encouraged in children's voices if we are serious about producing, in time, truly singing congregations. Augustine's words still remind us: "Those who sing, pray twice!"

Helping People Sing
and Other Music Matters

Sometimes we seem to face a nonsinging assembly—children or adults or both. The problem can usually be overcome with certain careful steps.

First, the assembly needs to know well the selections to be sung. A vague familiarity from hearing a piece once or twice is not enough. When new music is introduced, it should be taught to the assembly. This is best done by someone (a music teacher often) who knows and can sing the piece reasonably well, "lining it out" one phrase at a time so that it can be echoed by those learning it. Repetition, sometimes much repetition, is needed so that the melody will be remembered. In the process, all stanzas of a song can be covered. This not only helps teach the melody, it brings out the unfamiliar words and gives everyone a first sense for the text. And that text is important—all of it. These texts are, in fact, the words of the liturgy. With them, the assembly can celebrate its liturgy. So words and melodies need to be introduced, taken in, made one's own. When no teacher for a new song is available, a recording can be used but never with quite the same good result. Often a combination of a teacher and a recording works well. In the classroom situation, this may often be a possibility.

Second, the assembly must be well led in its song. This is best done by the organist, pianist or other instrumentalist. This person is not really an "accompanist" but a leader of song. The manner of performance, regardless of the instrument being played, must be assertive, rhythmic and predictable. Introductions must be long enough to permit everyone to locate the page (when the piece is a new hymn), and must make it clear at just what moment the introduction is over and the singing is to begin. If no competent instrumentalist is available, the next best answer is a competent singer to act as song leader. Whenever possible, this leader should work without a mike so that the leader's voice does not overwhelm and suppress the song of the assembly.

Third, the assembly needs to realize that singing is not window dressing but *is* their prayer, their liturgy. This is greatly enhanced when music is chosen out of clear understanding of how each bit of singing works within the liturgy. In the case of a hymn, its sound and its words become a part of how the assembly celebrates the liturgy. The hymn is not there to cover empty time but to be our deed. More often than not, this means that very good reasons are necessary before omitting any stanzas of a hymn. If the text forms a whole, it should be treated as such.

STUDYING THE HYMNS

Those who prepare the liturgy and its music should know how to find and use information about hymns.

In the *Hymnal for Catholic Students*, as in some other hymnals, the notes in small type below each hymn provide information about the words (top line) and the tune (bottom line). For example, below "Alleluia, sing to Jesus" we find:

Text: Rev. 5:9; William C. Dix, 1837–1898
Tune: HYFRYDOL, 8 7 8 7 D; Rowland H. Prichard, 1811–1887

The "text" line tells us that the words were written by William C. Dix who was born in 1837 and died in 1898. He based these words on images and ideas found in the book of Revelation. When the text of a hymn was originally written in another language, the original title appears first, followed by the name of the author and then the translator.

The "tune" line tells us that the melody was written by Rowland H. Prichard who lived about the same time as William Dix. It tells us also that Prichard called his tune HYFRYDOL, a Welsh word meaning "good cheer." Composers of hymn tunes usually name each tune. The name may be a city or other place, a person or some name that may have meaning to the composer alone. This name then identifies the tune to musicians. It makes it easy to identify a tune *as a tune* apart from any set of words.

Some of the information on the "tune" line refers to both words and music. In this case, it is the numbers (8 7 8 7) and the letter (D). These numbers mean that the first line of this hymn has eight syllables, the second line has seven syllables, the third line eight again, the fourth line seven. The "D" means "doubled": the same pattern is repeated so that each whole verse of the hymn has eight lines and that these lines alternate between eight and seven syllables. This information can be very useful. Sometimes in preparing the liturgy, a hymn is found whose words are perfect to the occasion. But no one knows its melody. Perhaps "Alleluia, sing to Jesus" has just been identified as the perfect text for the closing hymn on Ascension Day, but no one has sung HYFRYDOL before and there is no time to teach it. However, a quick look through the hymnal would turn up at least one other hymn with the 8 7 8 7 D pattern. This is "Lord, you give the great commission." The tune for this hymn has the name HYMN TO JOY. The assembly may know how to sing "Lord, you give the great commission" very well to this tune. In that case, "Alleluia, sing to Jesus" can be sung on Ascension, not to HYFRYDOL but to the tune people associate with "Lord, you give the great commission." But perhaps no one has ever sung "Lord, you give the great commission" either. At this point, someone may recognize that HYMN TO JOY is a tune everyone knows from singing "Joyful, joyful we adore thee" at Sunday Mass. So the day is saved. (The accompaniment edition to the *Hymnal for Catholic Students* has an index of all the tunes. This will list the various patterns such as 8 7 8 7 D and then give all the tunes in the book that have this pattern.)

Singing new or unfamiliar texts to old, well-known tunes has a long history in music and in worship. Not every combination of words and music will work simply because the syllable pattern is the same. Some melodies just do not fit the character of the words. Try, for example, to sing "Joy to the world" to the tune called NEW BRITAIN (which many know from "Amazing grace"). It can be done, but the festive character of the words does not fit the subdued melody. Words and tune need to be at home with each other.

PSALMS AND CANTORS

The psalms are the book of prayers of Jews and Christians. Though we have added many other prayers over the centuries, we continue to return to this source. There are 150 psalms in the book of Psalms in the Bible. It is clear that many of these were originally sung. That tradition has continued. Sometimes an entire psalm is sung by everyone. Often, though, the church uses a method that is less demanding. This is "responsorial" psalm singing. In this method, which has become very common at the Sunday Mass for the psalm after the first reading, the assembly sings only a single line (usually taken directly from the psalm). This becomes a refrain and its music is the only music the assembly needs to learn. The rest of the psalm is sung by a cantor or by a choir, with the assembly coming in to sing the refrain after each stanza. When neither cantor nor choir are available, the verses of the psalm can be read by one person. Even when this happens, it is still appropriate that the refrain be sung after each verse or stanza.

When the verses are sung, the words must be understood by all. In the case of a children's liturgy, this usually means that the cantor should be an adult (perhaps one of the parish's cantors or a music teacher or the organist). Some older children, however, especially those with experience in a choir, are quite successful as cantors and should be nurtured in this role.

Note that the role of cantor is not the same as that of song leader. The cantor leads psalms and litanies (the intercessions, some forms of the Agnus Dei and the penitential rite) and sometimes other compositions in which the assembly sings only a refrain or chorus. The cantor may also function as a song leader, but the two roles are very different. A song leader takes the place of the instrumentalist when necessary (as mentioned above) and sings what the assembly sings. The cantor sings alone, usually in a back-and-forth pattern with the assembly.

COPYRIGHTS

The approach to children's liturgies taken in this book makes it clear that most of the music at a liturgy and everything that the assembly recites is meant to be known by heart. This includes the spoken responses to the presider, acclamations like the alleluia and the memorial acclamation, litanies like the Agnus Dei. It is hoped that the *Hymnal for Catholic Students* will most often be adequate to provide the students with the words and music they need for hymns and chants that are used only occasionally and so must be followed in some printed form. When additional words and music must be reproduced for use by the assembly, the proper permissions should always be obtained from the copyright owners. Some publishers offer license agreements that will cover multiple uses over a given period of time. In any case, the copyright information must be included on the participation aid. For additional information on copyrights, see the appendix to *The Welcome Table: Planning Masses with Children* (published by Liturgy Training Publications).

Index of Music

All references are to page numbers in the *Hymnal for Catholic Students.*

CHRISTMAS/EPIPHANY

COMMUNION PROCESSIONALS

CONFIRMATION

PRAYER TO END THE DAY

PRESENTATION OF THE LORD (FEBRUARY 2)

SANCTUS

SCHOOL YEAR: CLOSING

SCHOOL YEAR: OPENING

Times of Mourning (Death, Funeral, Memorial)

Unity